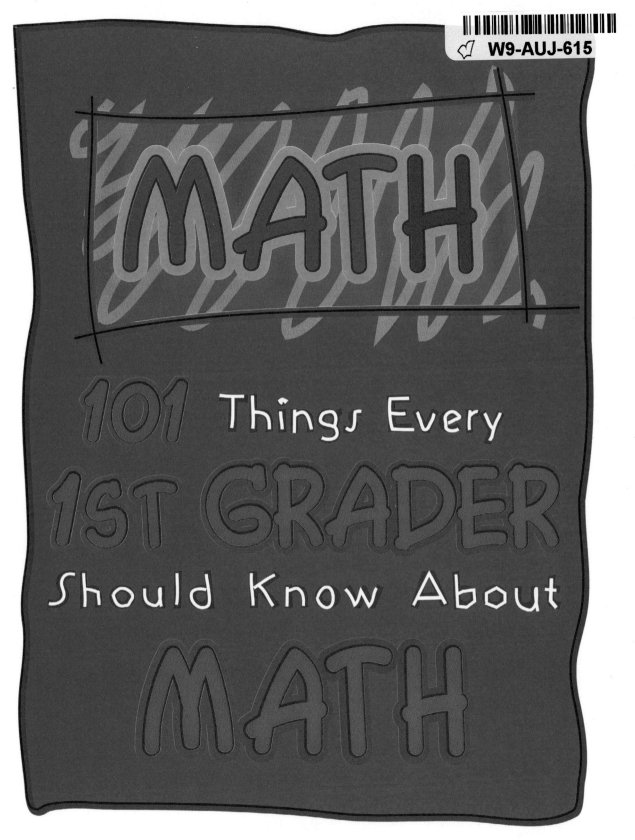

MATH

101 Things Every 1ST GRADER Should Know About MATH

Peg Hall

Consultant: Elizabeth C. Stull, Ph.D.

active minds®

Writer: Peg Hall has written numerous teacher guides and student activity books, as well as fiction and nonfiction books for children. Her career has included experience as a classroom and reading resource teacher, editor, and education consultant. Ms. Hall currently works as a freelance writer from her home in coastal Massachusetts.

Consultant: Elizabeth C. Stull holds a doctorate in early and middle childhood education specializing in curriculum. She has taught language, literacy, and children's literature at Ohio State University and has written numerous activity books for teachers, including *Alligators to Zebras: Whole Language Activities for the Primary Grades, Kindergarten Teacher's Survival Guide,* and *Multicultural Learning Activities: K–6.*

Illustrations: George Ulrich.

Louis Weber, CEO
Publications International, Ltd.
7373 North Cicero Avenue
Lincolnwood, Illinois 60712

www.myactiveminds.com

ISBN-13: 978-1-4127-1235-4
ISBN-10: 1-4127-1235-1

Manufactured in China.

8 7 6 5 4 3 2 1

Contents

Add Some Fun to Math

Dear Parents:

Starting 1st grade is an exciting time for children. They know the basics of reading, writing, and math and are ready for new challenges. They seem to want to know more about everything! Of course you want to give your child that special head start that is so important. This workbook will help your child learn the basic skills of a vast array of math concepts and processes—skills your child will build on in future learning.

Inside this workbook, children will find 101 fun-filled math activities right at their fingertips. Each activity focuses on a different skill and provides your child with plenty of opportunity to practice that skill. The activities are arranged in order of difficulty, beginning with the most basic skills to build your child's confidence as he or she goes along. They'll feel a real sense of accomplishment as they complete each page.

Every activity is clearly labeled with the skill being taught. You will find skill keys written especially for you, the parent, at the bottom of each activity page. These skill keys give you information about what your child is learning. Also, suggestions are provided for additional hands-on activities you may choose to do with your child.

These offer fun, enjoyable opportunities to reinforce the skill being taught.

Children learn in a variety of ways. They are sure to appreciate the bright, exciting illustrations in this workbook. The pictures are not just fun—they also help visual learners develop their math skills by giving them something to relate to. Children may also like to touch and trace the numbers and pictures and say them out loud. Each method can be an important aid in your child's learning process.

Your child can tackle some of the activities independently; in other cases you will need to read the directions for your child before he or she can complete the exercise. Each activity should be fun and enough of a challenge that it will be exciting for your child. Be patient, and support your child in positive ways. Let them know it's all right to take a guess or pull back if they're unsure. And, of course, celebrate their successes with them.

Learning should be an exciting and positive experience for everyone. Enjoy your time together as your child enhances his or her 1st-grade math skills.

Counting On a Prize

It's almost time for the big race. Count the prizes in each set.
Circle the number that tells how many.

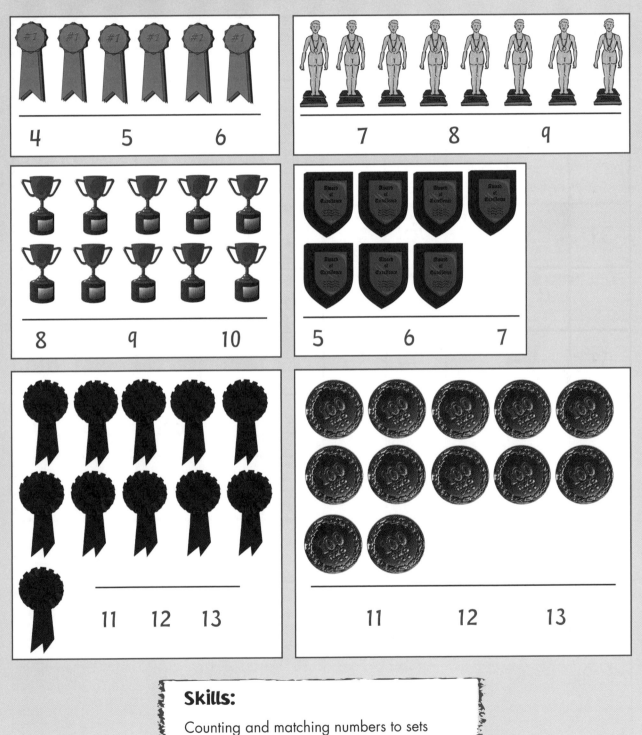

4   5   6

7   8   9

8   9   10

5   6   7

11   12   13

11   12   13

Skills:

Counting and matching numbers to sets

Answers on page 121.

Race and Write

Some numbers are missing. Write each number where it belongs.

1	2		4	5		7	8		10
	12	13		15			18	19	
		23	24			27	28		30
31			34	35			38	39	
	42			45	46			49	
51			54	55				59	60
	62	63			66		68		70
	72		74	75		77			80
81		83					88	89	
	92	93		95			98		100

Skills:

Identifying and writing missing numbers to 100

8

Answers on page 121.

Time to Shape Up!

Color the shapes below to show which caterpillar will lift them.

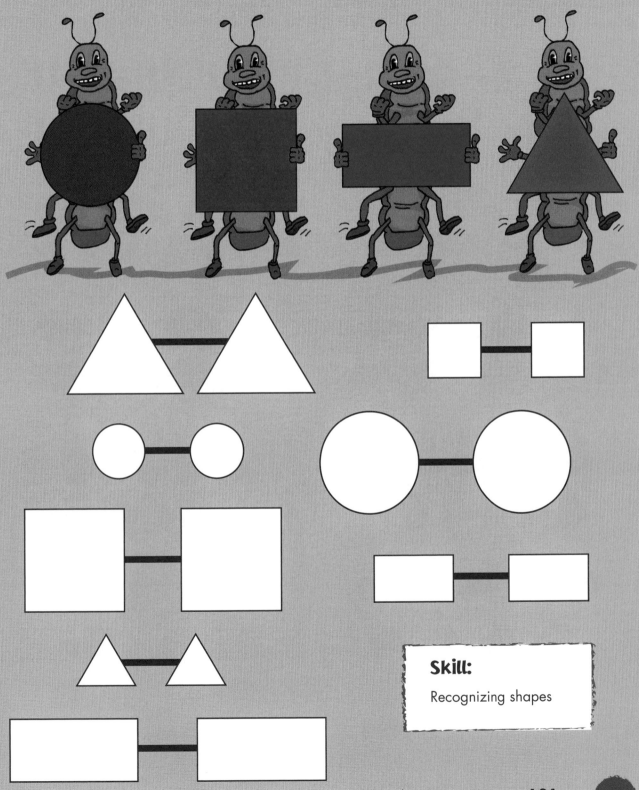

Skill:

Recognizing shapes

Answers on page 121.

Hats Off!

Equivalent sets have an equal number of things. Draw lines from Column A to Column B to connect equivalent sets.

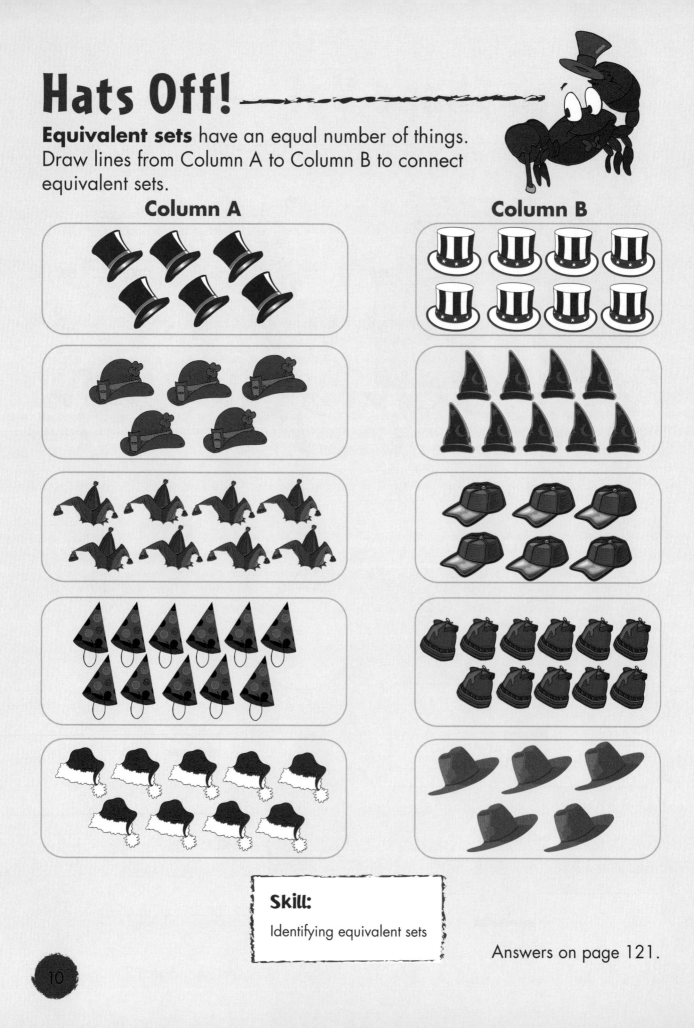

Column A

Column B

Skill:

Identifying equivalent sets

Answers on page 121.

All in a Row

Write the numbers that are missing.

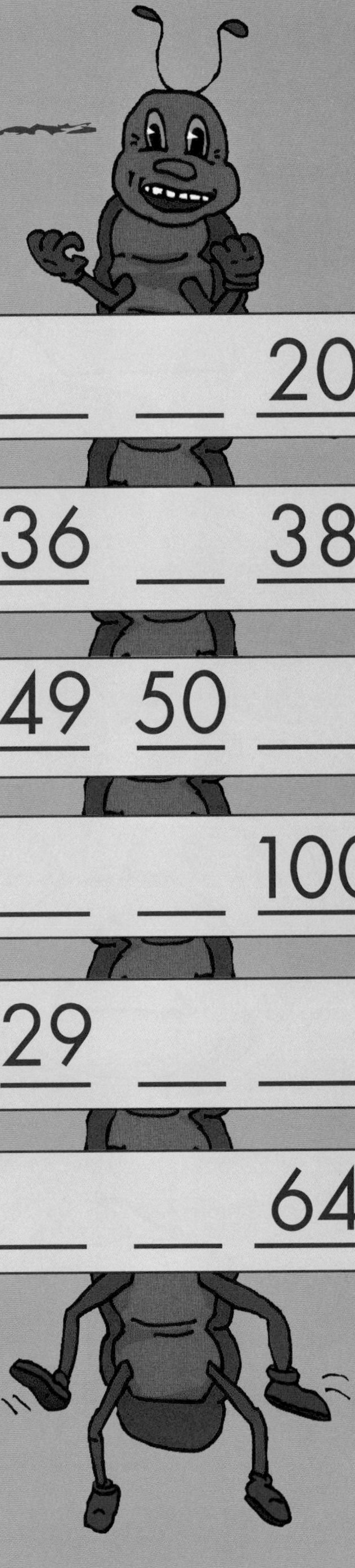

13 14 ___ 16 17 ___ ___ 20

31 ___ 33 34 ___ 36 ___ 38

___ 45 46 ___ 48 49 50 ___

93 ___ ___ 96 97 ___ ___ 100

24 ___ 26 ___ 28 29 ___ ___

___ 58 ___ ___ 61 ___ ___ 64

Skill:

Writing missing numbers on a number line

Answers on page 121.

Baggage Check

Skill:

Sorting by attributes

The animals are looking for their bags. Use the shapes to match each animal to its bag. Write each animal's name on the correct tag.

The Wrong Bag

Look at each set of bags. Circle the one that does not belong.

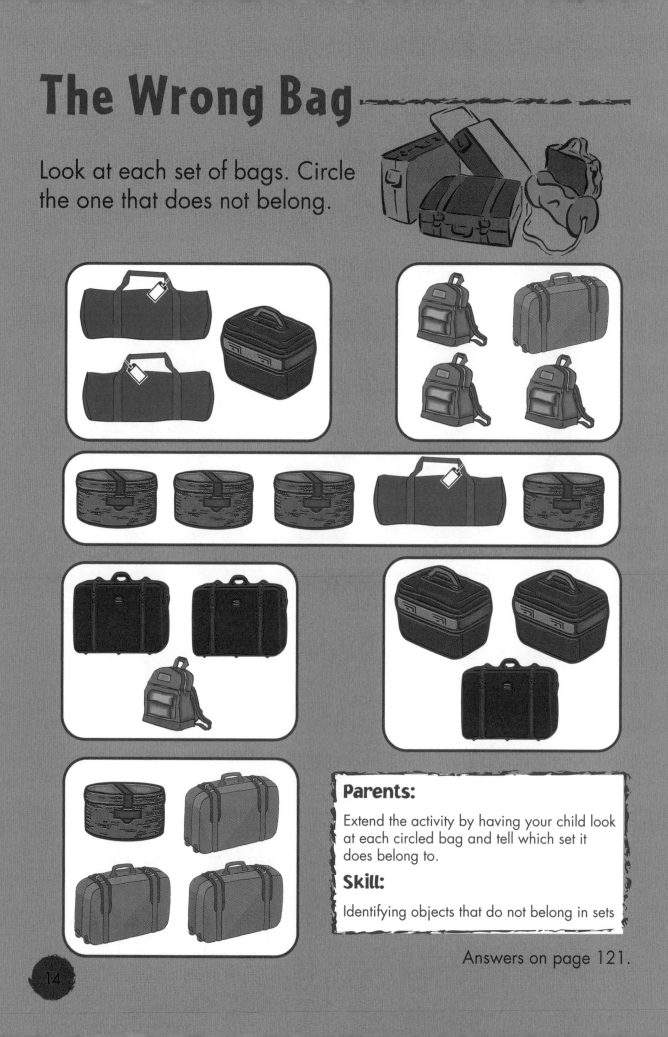

Parents:

Extend the activity by having your child look at each circled bag and tell which set it does belong to.

Skill:

Identifying objects that do not belong in sets

Answers on page 121.

14

Sort the Bags!

Look at the bags. Put them into different kinds of sets.

Find a set of red bags. Put **X** on each bag in the set.

Find a set of yellow bags. Put ✔ on each bag in the set.

Find a set of green bags. Put a ☐ around each bag in the set.

Find a set of backpacks. Put a ◯ around each bag in the set.

Skill:

Sorting by subsets

Answers on page 121.

Camp Pictures

Jan wants to draw pictures of things she saw on her trip. Follow the directions to help her.

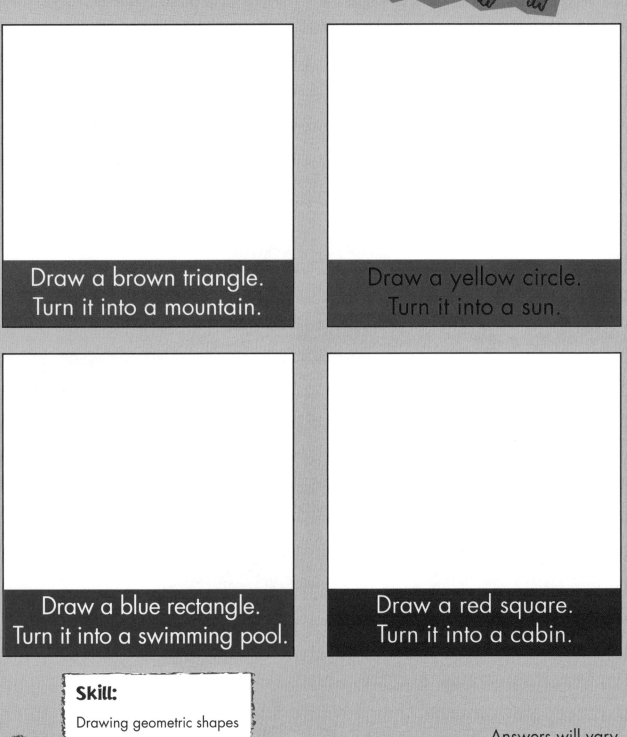

Draw a brown triangle.
Turn it into a mountain.

Draw a yellow circle.
Turn it into a sun.

Draw a blue rectangle.
Turn it into a swimming pool.

Draw a red square.
Turn it into a cabin.

Skill:

Drawing geometric shapes

Answers will vary.

Shape Match

Think about each shape. Draw a line to show which object has the same shape.

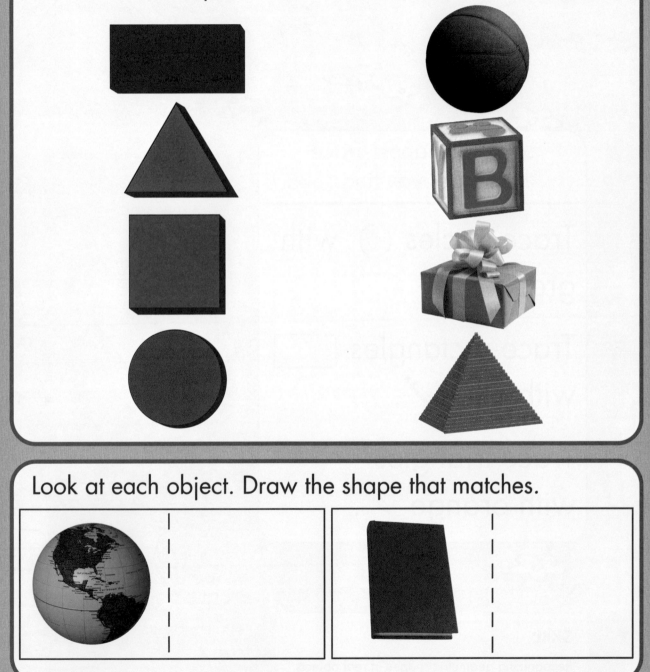

Look at each object. Draw the shape that matches.

Skill:

Matching two-dimensional and three-dimensional shapes

Answers on page 121.

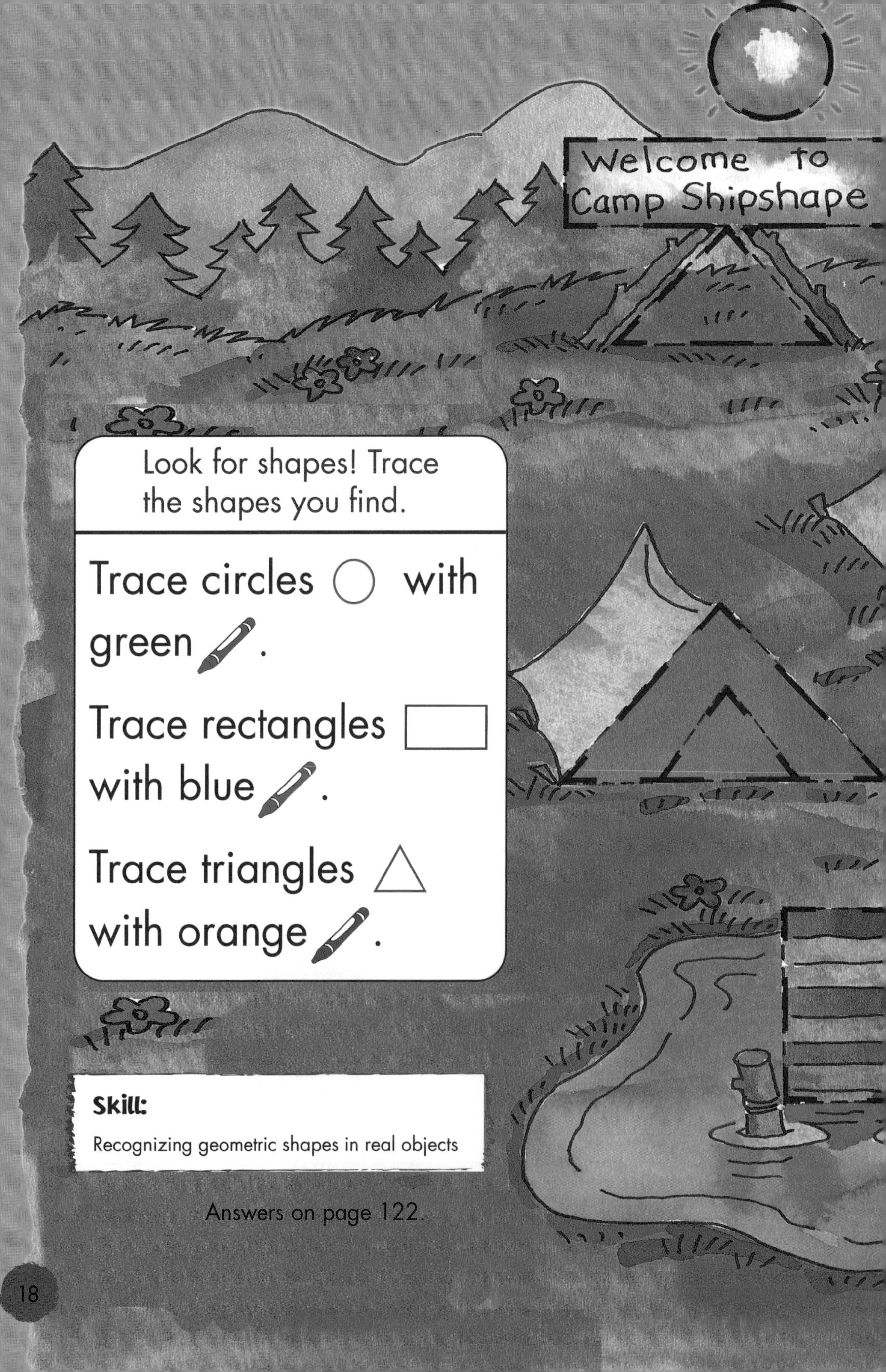

Welcome to Camp Shipshape

Look for shapes! Trace the shapes you find.

Trace circles ◯ with green ✏.

Trace rectangles ▭ with blue ✏.

Trace triangles △ with orange ✏.

Skill:

Recognizing geometric shapes in real objects

Answers on page 122.

Searching Camp "Shipshape"

More or Less?

Write the numbers on the lines.

The big clown has _____ apples.

4 is less than 6.

The big clown has **less.**

The little clown has _____ apples.

6 is more than 4.

The little clown has **more.**

Circle the clown who has **more.**

Circle the clown who has **more** balloons. Write the numbers on the lines.

_____ is more than _____.

Circle the monkey who has **more** bananas. Write the numbers on the lines.

_____ is more than _____.

Circle the seal who has **less** balls.

_____ is less than _____.

Skill:

Understanding **more** and **less**

20

Answers on page 122.

The Greatest Show on Earth!

Read each sign. Circle the animal it tells about.

SEE THE BIGGEST LION!

SEE THE TALLEST BEAR!

SEE THE SMALLEST ELEPHANT!

SEE THE LONGEST SEAL!

SEE THE MEDIUM-SIZE HORSE!

Skill:

Comparing by size

Answers on page 122.

Tricks of the Trade

The animals are learning some new tricks. Circle the word that tells about each trick.

The ball is
on   under
the seal's nose.

The tiger is jumping
over   under
the box.

The pony is
beside   between
the elephants.

The whale is
over   under
the ball.

The monkeys are
between
in front of
the man.

The monkey is
in
on
the car.

Skill:

Understanding positional words

Answers on page 122.

On the Scale

A scale is used to measure weight. Look at the numbers on the scale to read the weight.

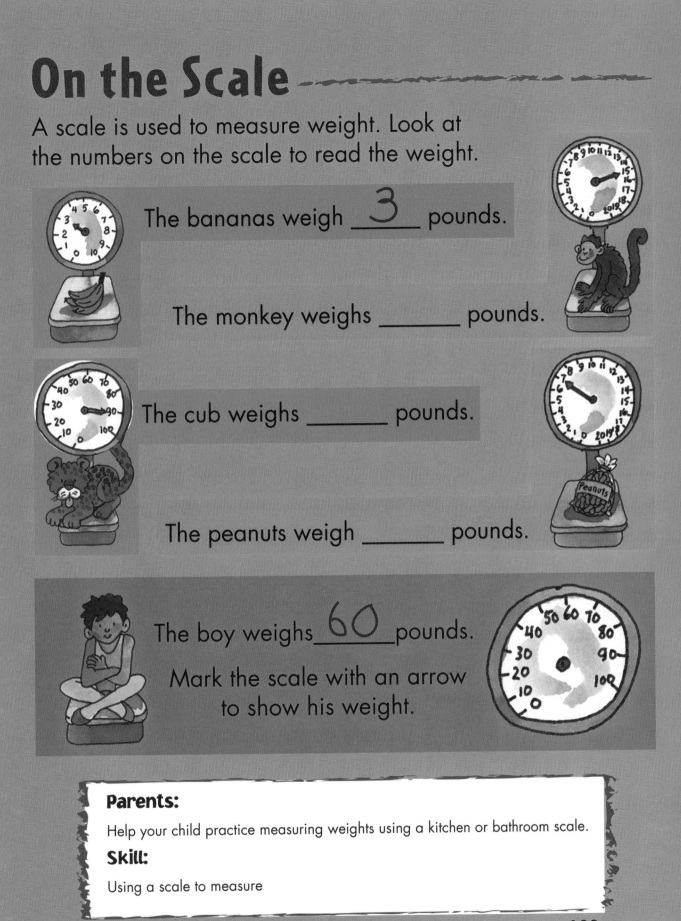

The bananas weigh __3__ pounds.

The monkey weighs _____ pounds.

The cub weighs _____ pounds.

The peanuts weigh _____ pounds.

The boy weighs __60__ pounds.

Mark the scale with an arrow to show his weight.

Parents:

Help your child practice measuring weights using a kitchen or bathroom scale.

Skill:

Using a scale to measure

Answers on page 122.

Find the Heavyweights

The elephant weighs **more** than the monkey.

The monkey weighs **less** than the elephant.

Circle the thing that weighs more.

Draw something that weighs **less**.

Skill:

Comparing by weight

Answers on page 122.

Monkey Measures

Count the tickets to measure.

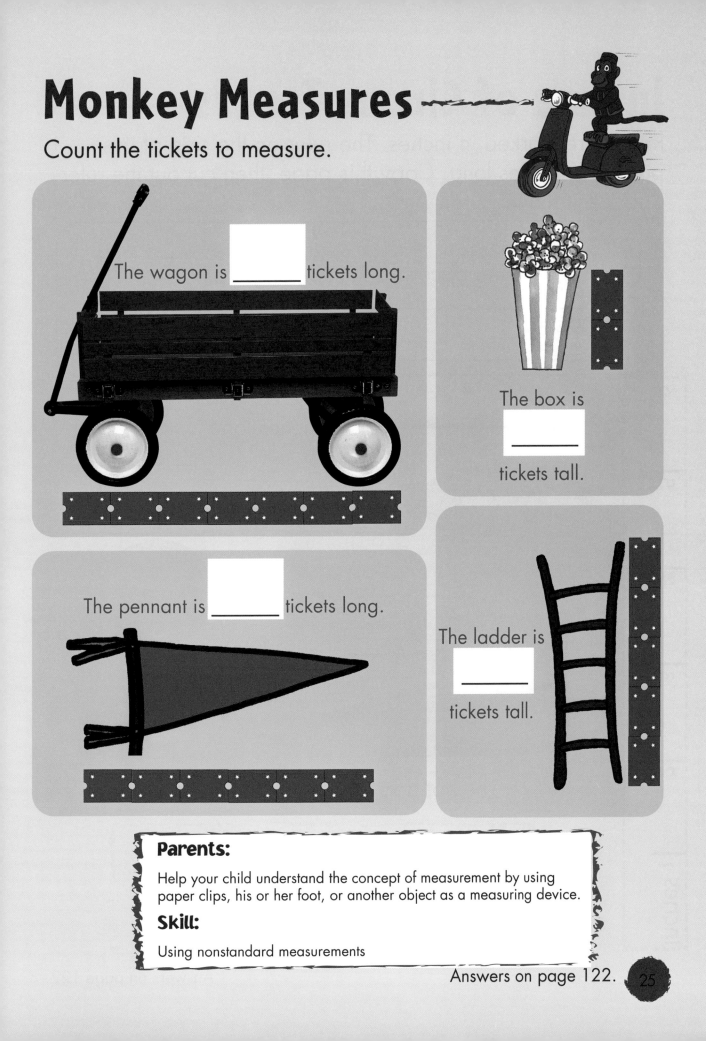

The wagon is _____ tickets long.

The box is _____ tickets tall.

The pennant is _____ tickets long.

The ladder is _____ tickets tall.

Parents:

Help your child understand the concept of measurement by using paper clips, his or her foot, or another object as a measuring device.

Skill:

Using nonstandard measurements

Answers on page 122.

Inches of Circus Treats

Rulers are marked in inches. The ruler on the side of this page is 6 inches long. Copy this page, then cut out the ruler and use it to measure.

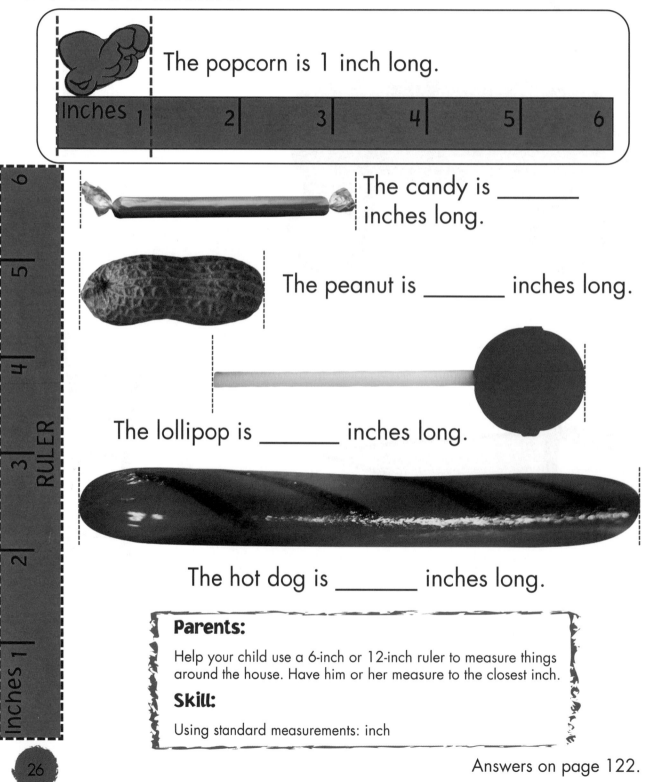

The popcorn is 1 inch long.

Inches 1 2 3 4 5 6

The candy is _____ inches long.

The peanut is _____ inches long.

The lollipop is _____ inches long.

The hot dog is _____ inches long.

Inches 1 2 3 4 5 6 RULER

Answers on page 122.

Measuring Up

Use the ruler from page 26 to draw some lines.

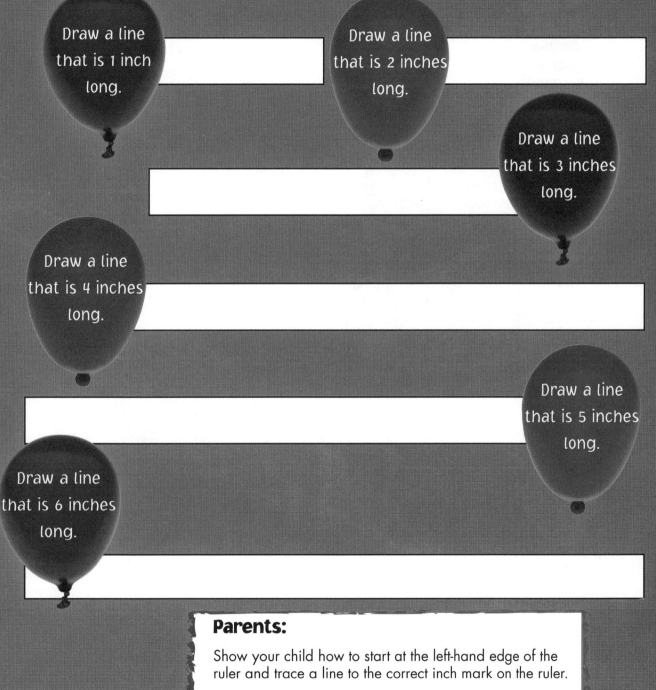

Draw a line that is 1 inch long.

Draw a line that is 2 inches long.

Draw a line that is 3 inches long.

Draw a line that is 4 inches long.

Draw a line that is 5 inches long.

Draw a line that is 6 inches long.

Parents:

Show your child how to start at the left-hand edge of the ruler and trace a line to the correct inch mark on the ruler.

Skill:

Drawing lines to specific measurements: inch

Answers on page 122.

Inches and Feet

One foot is the same as 12 inches. Circle the measurement that tells how long each thing probably is.

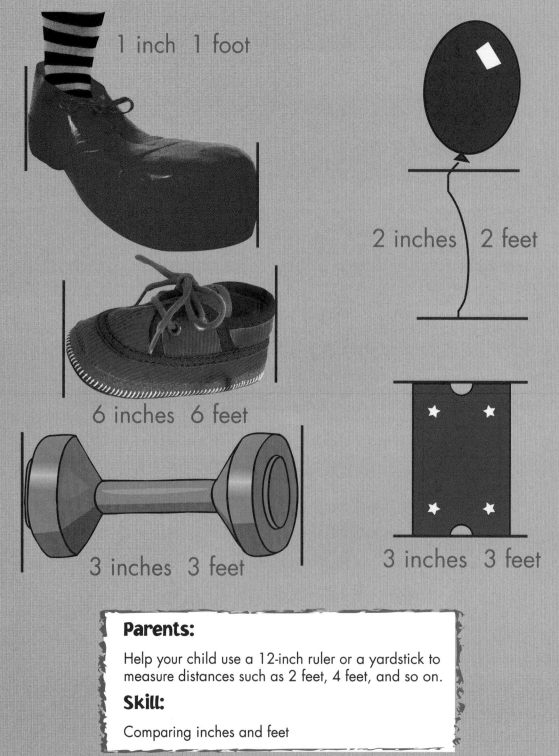

1 inch   1 foot

2 inches   2 feet

6 inches   6 feet

3 inches   3 feet

3 inches   3 feet

Parents:

Help your child use a 12-inch ruler or a yardstick to measure distances such as 2 feet, 4 feet, and so on.

Skill:

Comparing inches and feet

Answers on page 122.

Counting Centimeters

Some rulers are marked in centimeters. The ruler on this page is 15 centimeters long. Copy this page, then cut out the ruler and use it to measure.

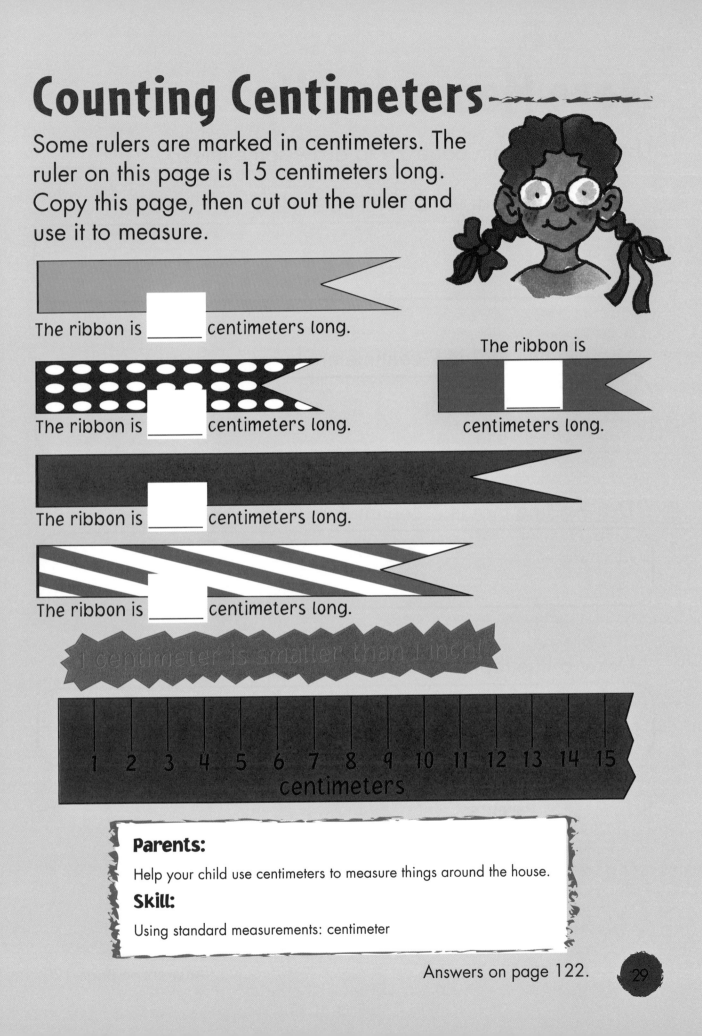

The ribbon is _____ centimeters long.

The ribbon is _____ centimeters long.

The ribbon is _____ centimeters long.

The ribbon is _____ centimeters long.

The ribbon is _____ centimeters long.

1 centimeter is smaller than 1 inch!

| 1 | 2 | 3 | 4 | 5 | 6 | 7 | 8 | 9 | 10 | 11 | 12 | 13 | 14 | 15 |
centimeters

Parents:

Help your child use centimeters to measure things around the house.

Skill:

Using standard measurements: centimeter

Answers on page 122.

More Measuring Up

Use the ruler from page 29 to draw some lines.

Draw a line that is 15 centimeters long.

Draw a line that is 9 centimeters long.

Draw a line that is 3 centimeters long.

Draw a line that is 12 centimeters long.

Parents:

Show your child how to start at the left-hand edge of the ruler and trace a line to the correct centimeter mark on the ruler.

Skill:

Drawing lines to specific measurements: centimeter

Answers on page 123.

Map Measuring

Use the distance scale to figure out how far.

EXAMPLE

It is __9__ feet from the

swings 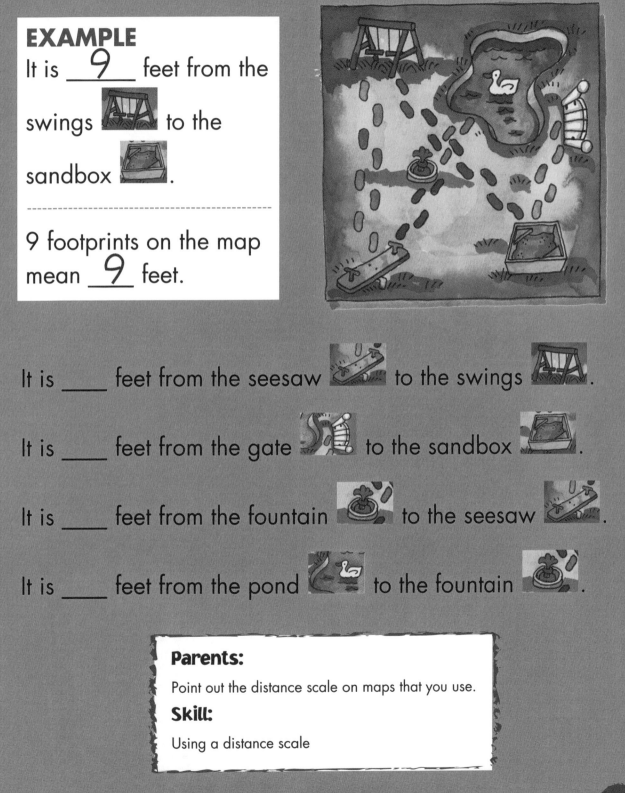 to the

sandbox .

----

9 footprints on the map
mean __9__ feet.

It is ____ feet from the seesaw to the swings .

It is ____ feet from the gate to the sandbox .

It is ____ feet from the fountain to the seesaw .

It is ____ feet from the pond to the fountain .

Parents:

Point out the distance scale on maps that you use.

Skill:

Using a distance scale

Counting Tag

Tag! You're It! Count backward to 0 before you peek.

30 _____ _____ _____ _____

_____ _____ _____ _____

_____ _____ _____ 0 _____

Skill:

Ordering descending numbers from 30

Answers on page 123.

32

Playing With Numbers

Write the numbers that come before and after.

40

42

___	33	___
___	65	___
___	10	___
___	49	___

___	30	___
___	99	___
___	21	___
___	84	___

Parents:

Give your child extra practice by saying a number and having him or her supply the number that comes before or after.

Skill:

Identifying numbers before and after a number

Answers on page 123.

Who's Number One?

Read the number words. Write the players' numbers on their shirts.

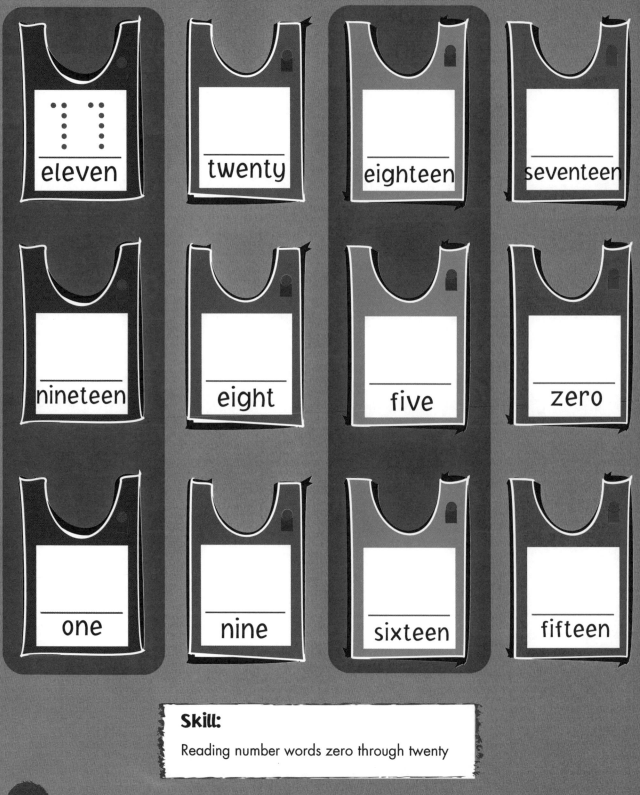

eleven

twenty

eighteen

seventeen

nineteen

eight

five

zero

one

nine

sixteen

fifteen

Skill:

Reading number words zero through twenty

Answers on page 123.

Count by 10s!

You can count by 10s! Touch the numbers as you count. Fill in the missing numbers on each bus.

10 20 30 40 50 60 70 80 90 100

S C H O O L   B U S

20 ___ 40

___ 90 100

80 90 ___

60 ___ 80

50 ___ 70

30 40 ___

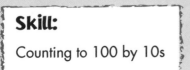

Skill:

Counting to 100 by 10s

Answers on page 123.

1	2	3	4	5	6	7	8	9	10
11	12	13	14	15	16	17	18	19	20
21	22	23	24	25	26	27	28	29	30
31	32	33	34	35	36	37	38	39	40
41	42	43	44	45	46	47	48	49	50
51	52	53	54	55	56	57	58	59	60
61	62	63	64	65	66	67	68	69	70
71	72	73	74	75	76	77	78	79	80
81	82	83	84	85	86	87	88	89	90
91	92	93	94	95	96	97	98	99	100

5

Look at the chart to count by 5s. Then count the train cars by 5s. Write the number next to each train car as you count.

Count by 5s

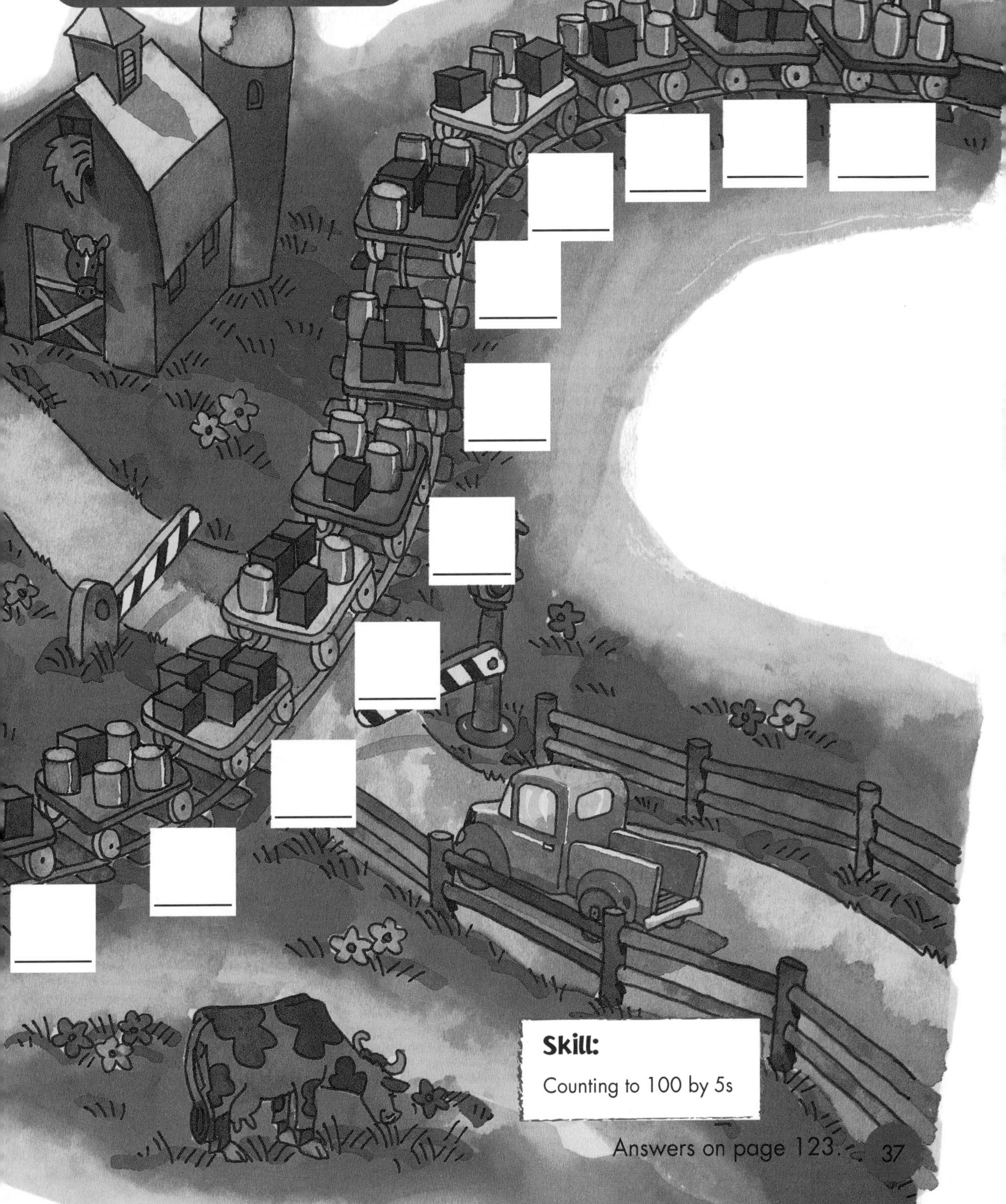

Skill:

Counting to 100 by 5s

Answers on page 123.

Traffic Patterns

Circle what comes next in each row.

Skills:

Recognizing and extending patterns

38

Answers on page 123.

Number Patterns

Numbers make patterns too.
Write the number that comes next in each set.

1	2	3	4	5	6	7	_____
2	4	6	8	10	12	14	_____
80	70	60	50	40	30	20	_____
5	10	15	20	25	30	35	_____

These patterns have numbers that repeat.

Can you figure out what comes next?

1	2	1	2	1	2	1	_____
2	3	4	2	3	4	2	_____
1	3	5	1	3	5	1	_____
2	2	3	3	4	4	5	_____

Skills:

Recognizing and extending number patterns

Answers on page 123.

Bus Stop

It's the bus driver's first day on the job. Draw a line to show him the way.

1st stop

2nd stop

3rd stop

4th stop

5th stop

6th stop

7th stop

8th stop

9th stop

10th stop

Parents:

Build your child's familiarity with ordinal numbers by using them in conversation. For example, "Today is August 12th."

Skill:

Recognizing ordinal numbers to 10th

Answers on page 123.

Number Word Match

Draw lines to match each race car with its trophy.

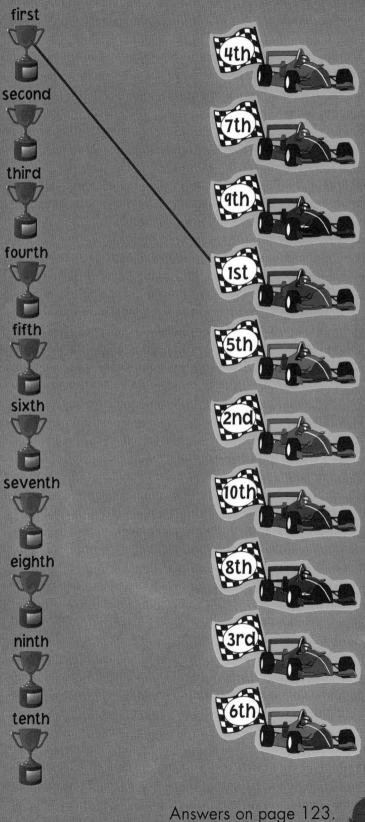

first

second

third

fourth

fifth

sixth

seventh

eighth

ninth

tenth

Parents:

Remind your child that looking for a smaller number word or part of the word can help when reading ordinal numbers. For example, find **four** in fourth, **fi** of five in fifth, **seven** in seventh, and so on.

Skill:

Matching ordinal numbers and number words

4th

7th

9th

1st

5th

2nd

10th

8th

3rd

6th

Wendy's Week

Trace the names of the days of the week.
Read to find out what Wendy will do.

Day of the Week	Things to Do
Sunday	Wash the dishes.
Monday	Make the bed.
Tuesday	Read a book.
Wednesday	Feed the cat.
Thursday	Play soccer.
Friday	Call Grandma.
Saturday	Go to the playground.

Draw lines to show what Wendy will do on each day.

Thursday   Sunday   Friday   Saturday   Tuesday

Skills:

Recognizing and reciting the days of the week in order

Answers on page 123.

Mixed-Up Months

Wendy dropped her calendar pages! Help her by writing the months in order.

July	September	March
October	January	April
August	February	December
June	november	May

1. <u>January</u>

2. _____

3. _____

4. _____

5. _____

6. _____

7. _____

8. _____

9. _____

10. _____

11. _____

12. _____

Parents:

Use the months to review seasons of the year. For example, ask which months are summer months, which are winter months, and so on.

Skills:

Recognizing and reciting the months of the year in order

Answers on page 123.

Wendy's Wonderful Month

August

Write the numbers that are missing from Wendy's calendar.

Sunday	Monday	Tuesday	Wednesday	Thursday
			1	2
5	☐	7	8	☐
☐	13	☐	☐	16
19	☐	21	22	☐
☐	27	☐	☐	30

Friday	Saturday
	11
	18
24	25
31	

Mark the important dates below on Wendy's calendar.

August 3rd
Swimming — Put an **S** on the day.

August 12th
Camping — Put a **C** on the day.

August 16th
Picnic — Put a **P** on the day.

August 20th
Races — Put an **R** on the day.

August 27th
Birthday party — Put a **B** on the day.

August 31st
Movies — Put an **M** on the day.

Skill:

Using a calendar

Picking Fruit

Put a ✓ beside the picture of your favorite fruit. Then ask 10 people to pick their favorite fruit, and put a ✓ beside it. Count how many ✓ marks you have for each fruit.

Fruit	Make ✓ marks.	Count the ✓ marks.
apple		
banana		
orange		
strawberry		
watermelon		

Skills:

Collecting and tallying data

Answers will vary.

Favorite Fruits

Use what you learned about people's favorite fruits on page 46 to make a graph.

Color in the squares to show how many times each fruit was picked.

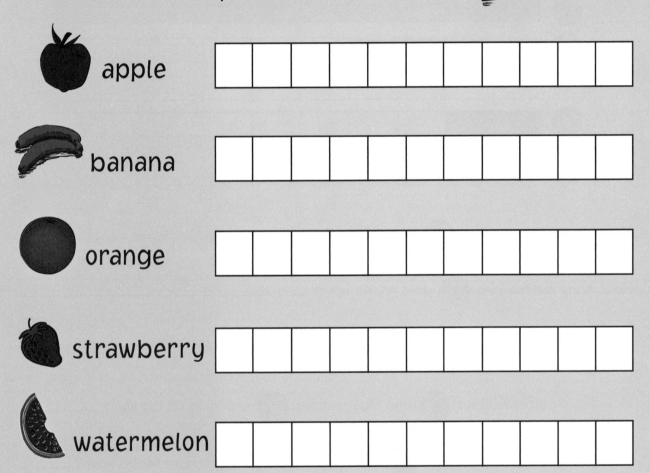

apple

banana

orange

strawberry

watermelon

Parents:

Have your child use the information from page 46 to complete this activity. For example, if he or she has 4 tally marks beside "apple," 4 squares in the apple row should be colored.

Skill:

Creating a pictograph

Marble Madness

Maria made a graph to keep track of her marbles.
Use the graph to answer the questions below.

number of marbles	1	2	3	4	5	6	7	8	9	10

How many green marbles does Maria have? _____

How many red marbles does Maria have? _____

Does Maria have more yellow marbles or more red marbles ? _____

How many purple marbles and blue marbles are there all together? _____

How many more green marbles than yellow marbles does Maria have? _____

How many more blue marbles than purple marbles does Maria have? _____

How many marbles does Maria have all together? _____

Skill:

Interpreting data from a bar graph

48

Answers on page 124.

Two Sides the Same

These shapes have two sides exactly the same.

Circle the things that have two sides exactly the same.

Skill:

Understanding symmetry

Answers on page 124.

Make Them the Same

Draw lines to make 2 sides that are exactly the same.

Answers on page 124.

Making Half

The whole circle is cut into 2 equal pieces.

Each piece is called a **half.**

Draw lines to cut the foods into 2 equal pieces.
Then color half of each food.

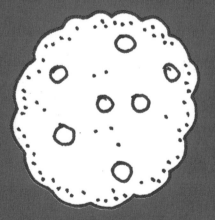

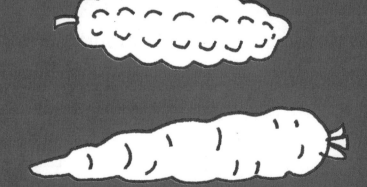

Skill:

Understanding whole and half

Answers on page 124.

Making Fourths

The whole circle is cut into 4 equal pieces.
Each piece is called a **fourth.**

Circle the shapes that show fourths.

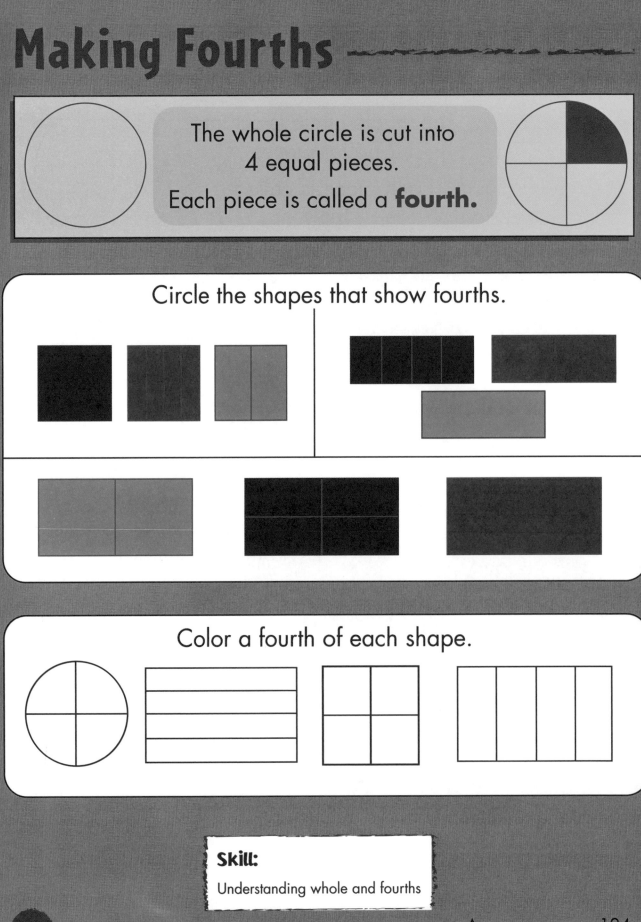

Color a fourth of each shape.

Skill:

Understanding whole and fourths

Answers on page 124.

Making Thirds

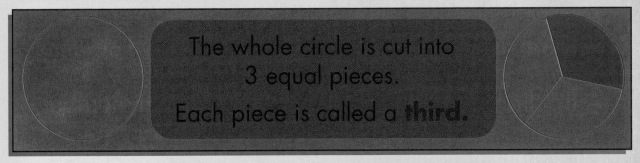

The whole circle is cut into
3 equal pieces.
Each piece is called a **third**.

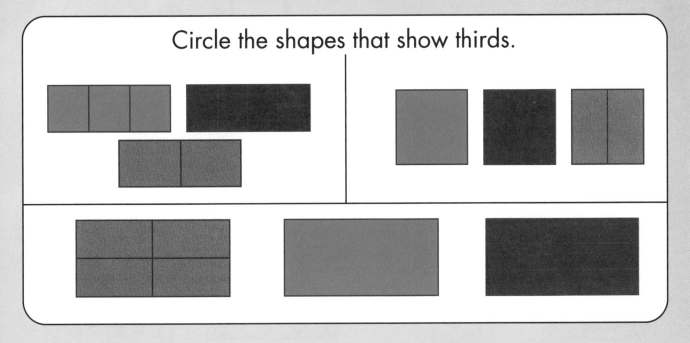

Circle the shapes that show thirds.

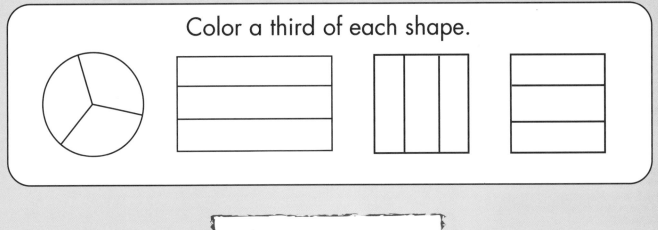

Color a third of each shape.

Skill:

Understanding whole and thirds

Answers on page 124.

Fantastic Fractions

The words **half, third,** and **fourth** tell about fractions.

Fractions are numbers that describe part of a whole thing.

A fraction has a top number and a bottom number.

The top number tells how many parts you have. →

The bottom number tells how many parts make up the whole thing. →

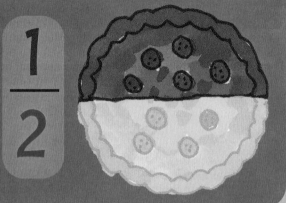

$\frac{1}{2}$

Count the pieces of pizza that are left.
Draw a line to the fraction.

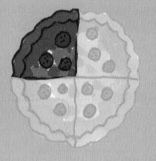 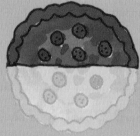 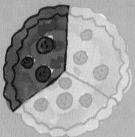 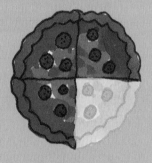

$\frac{1}{3}$ $\frac{1}{2}$ $\frac{3}{4}$ $\frac{1}{4}$

Skill:

Understanding fractional numbers

Answers on page 124.

More Fantastic Fractions

Count how many parts are left. $\underline{1}$

Count how many parts make a whole. $\underline{4}$

Write the fraction. $\dfrac{1}{4}$

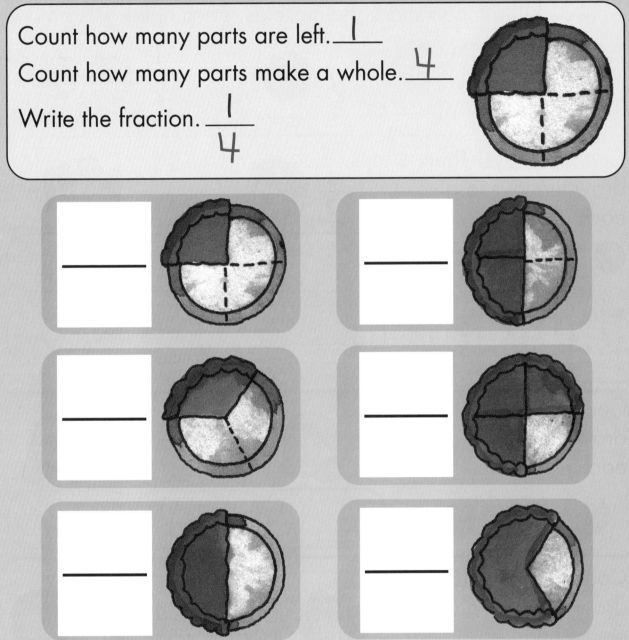

Answers on page 124.

Share and Share Alike

Two children can share the marbles. Each child gets half.

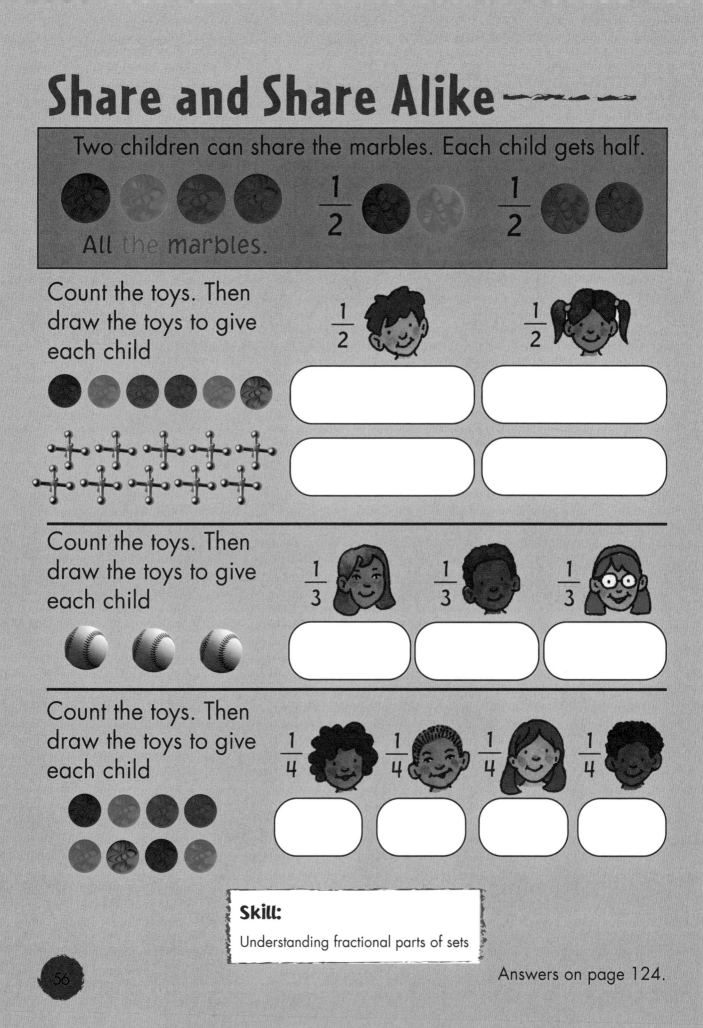

All the marbles. $\frac{1}{2}$ $\frac{1}{2}$

Count the toys. Then draw the toys to give each child

$\frac{1}{2}$ $\frac{1}{2}$

Count the toys. Then draw the toys to give each child

$\frac{1}{3}$ $\frac{1}{3}$ $\frac{1}{3}$

Count the toys. Then draw the toys to give each child

$\frac{1}{4}$ $\frac{1}{4}$ $\frac{1}{4}$ $\frac{1}{4}$

Skill:

Understanding fractional parts of sets

56

Answers on page 124.

Twelve at a Time!

Dozen is another name for 12 things.

Here are 1 dozen eggs. Number the eggs from 1 to 12.

Here is half a dozen. How many eggs are in $\frac{1}{2}$ dozen? _____

Circle a set of 1 dozen eggs.

Circle a set of $\frac{1}{2}$ dozen eggs.

Fill It Up!

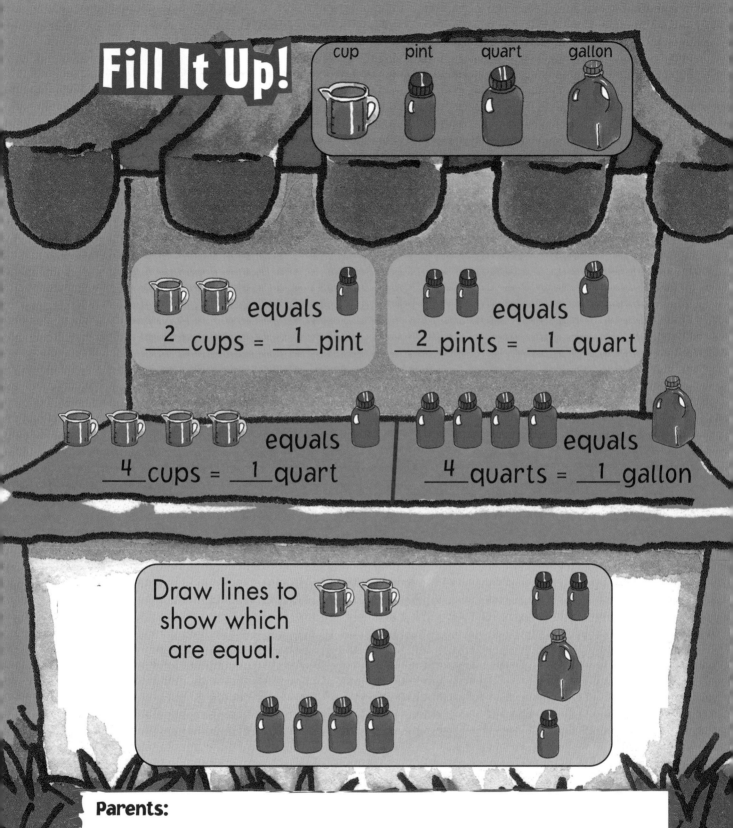

cup   pint   quart   gallon

equals

___2___ cups = ___1___ pint

equals

___2___ pints = ___1___ quart

equals

___4___ cups = ___1___ quart

equals

___4___ quarts = ___1___ gallon

Draw lines to show which are equal.

Parents:

Have your child experiment with filling and emptying cup, pint, quart, and gallon containers.

Skill:

Comparing volume/volume equivalents

Answers on page 124.

Taking Time

Look at the pictures below. Circle your answers.

Which takes more time?

Which takes more time?

Which takes more time?

Which takes more time?

Which takes more time?

Which takes more time?

Skill:

Comparing duration of time

Answers on page 124.

The Same Time

Time is measured in seconds, minutes, hours, and days.

1 day	is the same as	24 hours.
1 hour	is the same as	60 minutes.
1 minute	is the same as	60 seconds.

Circle your answers.

Which is more time?	1 day	1 minute
Which is more time?	60 seconds	1 hour
Which is more time?	2 hours	1 day
Which is more time?	30 seconds	1 hour
Which is more time?	24 days	24 hours

Look at the following activities.
Circle the time each probably takes.

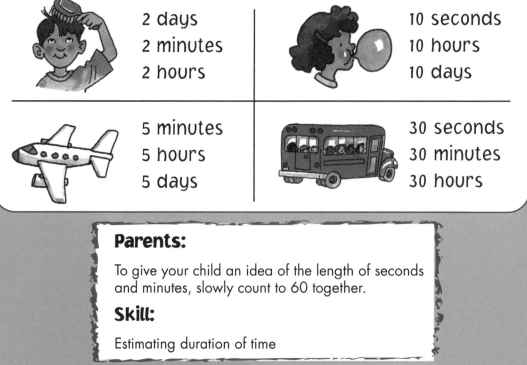

2 days 2 minutes 2 hours	10 seconds 10 hours 10 days
5 minutes 5 hours 5 days	30 seconds 30 minutes 30 hours

Parents:

To give your child an idea of the length of seconds and minutes, slowly count to 60 together.

Skill:

Estimating duration of time

Answers on page 124.

A Clock's Face

What has a face and hands but cannot smile or wave?

A clock!

Look at this clock's face and hands.

The clock has a short hour hand. Color the hour hand red.

The clock has a longer minute hand. Color the minute hand blue.

The clock has a long, thin second hand. Color the second hand green.

Skill:

Understanding a clock face

Answers on page 124.

What's the Hour?

The hands on a clock go around and around.

Each time the minute hand reaches 12, a whole hour has gone by.

The hour hand points to the new hour.

The hands on this clock show that it is 10 o'clock. Write it like this: 10:00.

Look at each clock.
Write the hour to show the time.

___:00   ___:00   ___:00

___:00   ___:00   ___:00

Skill:

Telling time to the hour

Answers on page 125.

Five Minutes More!

The hands on a clock go around and around.

Each number on the clock stands for 5 minutes.

Count by 5s to write the minutes next to the numbers.

Parents:

You may want to review counting by 5s before having your child complete the page.

Skill:

Counting minutes in increments of 5

Answers on page 125.

Halfway Around the Clock

When the minute hand gets to 6, it is halfway around the clock face. That means 30 minutes have gone by.

The hour hand is between 3:00 and 4:00.

The minute hand shows that 30 minutes have gone by.

The time on the clock is 3:30.

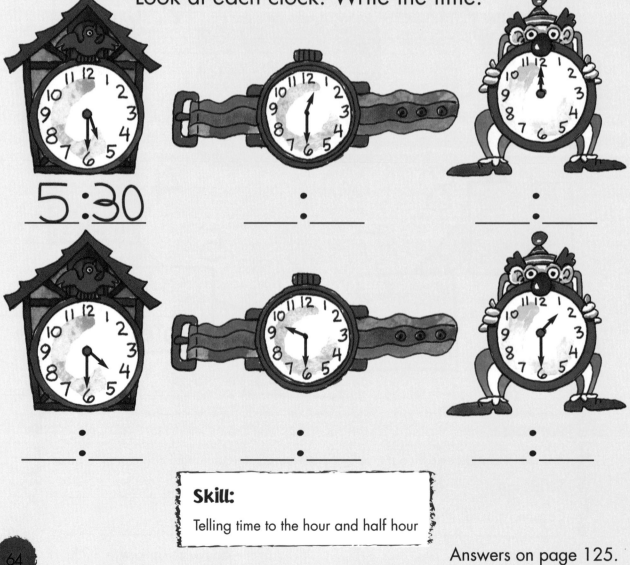

Look at each clock. Write the time.

5:30

___:___

___:___

___:___

___:___

___:___

Skill:

Telling time to the hour and half hour

64

Answers on page 125.

Clock Match

Draw lines to match the clocks that show the same time.

3:00   1:30   5:00   2:30   7:00

Write the time.

6:30   5:30

___:___   ___:___   ___:___

Skill:

Telling time on analog and digital clocks

Watch Out for Time!

Look at each watch. Draw a line to the time it shows.

6:00   7:00   2:00   2:30   7:30   1:00

Draw hands on the clocks to show the time.

8:00   8:30   11:30

Skill:

Telling time: review

66

Answers on page 125.

Count by 2s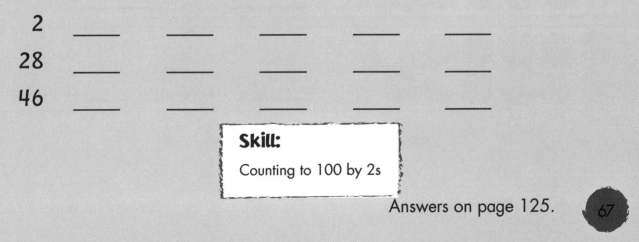

Write the missing numbers. Then say the numbers in the yellow spaces. You are counting by 2s!

1		3		5		7		9	10
11	12	13	14	15	16	17		19	
21		23		25	26	27	28	29	30
31		33	34	35		37		39	
41	42	43	44	45	46	47		49	
51	52	53		55	56	57	58	59	60
61		63	64	65		67		69	
71	72	73		75	76	77	78	79	80
81		83	84	85		87	88	89	
91	92	93		95	96	97		99	

Start with the first number and count by 2s.

2 ____ ____ ____ ____ ____

28 ____ ____ ____ ____ ____

46 ____ ____ ____ ____ ____

Skill:

Counting to 100 by 2s

Answers on page 125.

Even or Odd?

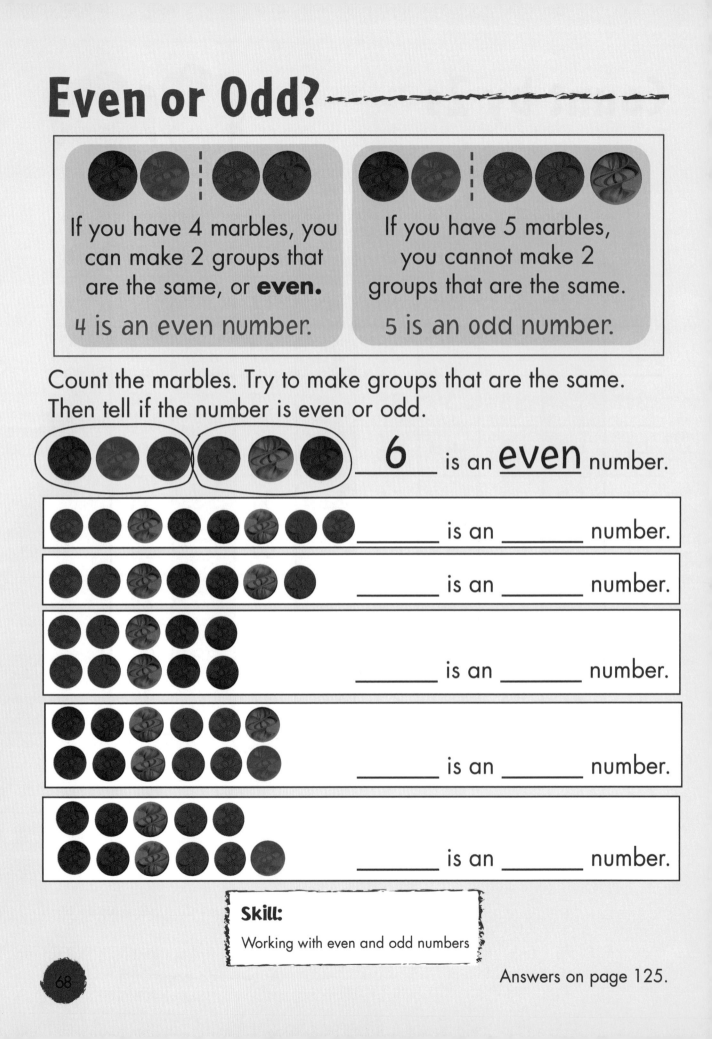

If you have 4 marbles, you can make 2 groups that are the same, or **even.**

4 is an even number.

If you have 5 marbles, you cannot make 2 groups that are the same.

5 is an odd number.

Count the marbles. Try to make groups that are the same.
Then tell if the number is even or odd.

___6___ is an **even** number.

_____ is an _____ number.

_____ is an _____ number.

_____ is an _____ number.

_____ is an _____ number.

_____ is an _____ number.

Skill:

Working with even and odd numbers

Answers on page 125.

How Many in All?

Adding is putting sets together.
You add to find out how many in all.

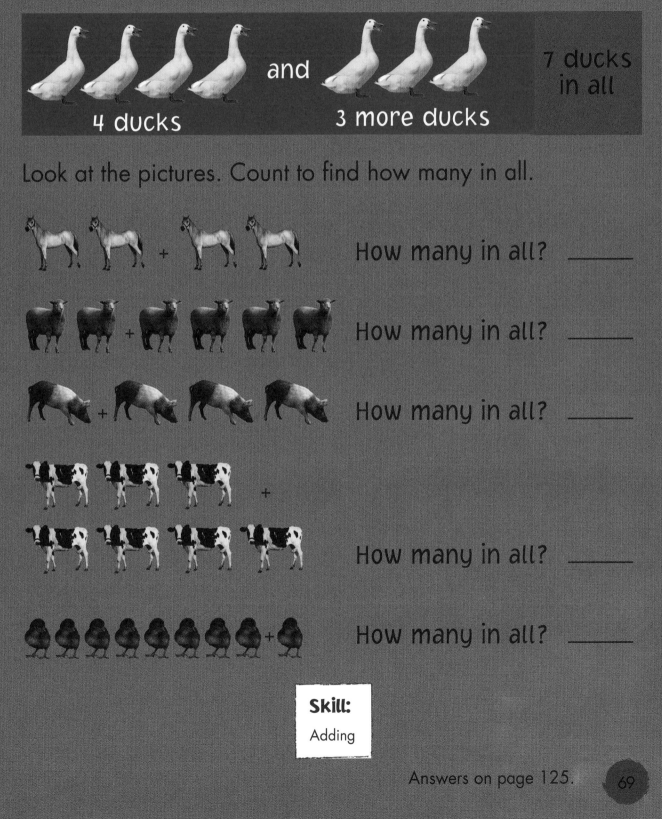

and

4 ducks

3 more ducks

7 ducks in all

Look at the pictures. Count to find how many in all.

+   How many in all? _____

+   How many in all? _____

+   How many in all? _____

+

How many in all? _____

+   How many in all? _____

Skill:

Adding

Add It Up!

Count the ducks to add.

Write a number sentence to tell how many in all.

Reading number sentences:
For + say "and" or "plus."
For = say "is" or "equals."

4 ducks   and   3 ducks   equals   7

4   +   3   =   7

Write the number for each set. Add to find how many in all.

_____ + _____ = _____

_____ + _____ = _____

_____ + _____ = _____

_____ + _____ = _____

_____ + _____ = _____

_____ + _____ = _____

Skills:

Combining sets to add using + and =

70

Answers on page 125.

Another Way to Add

These number facts have the same answer.

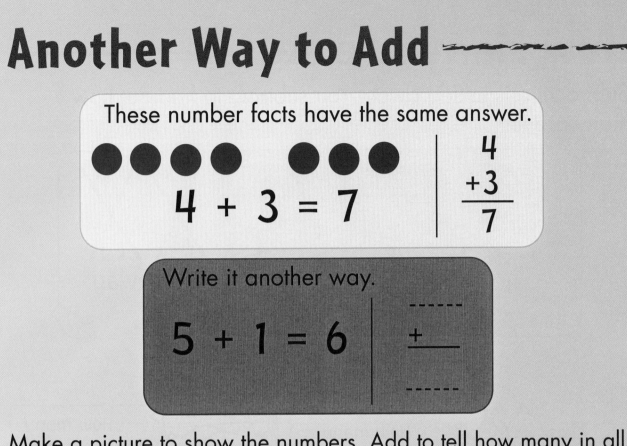

$$4 + 3 = 7$$

$$\begin{array}{r} 4 \\ +3 \\ \hline 7 \end{array}$$

Write it another way.

$$5 + 1 = 6$$

$$\begin{array}{r} \text{------} \\ + \\ \hline \text{------} \end{array}$$

Make a picture to show the numbers. Add to tell how many in all.

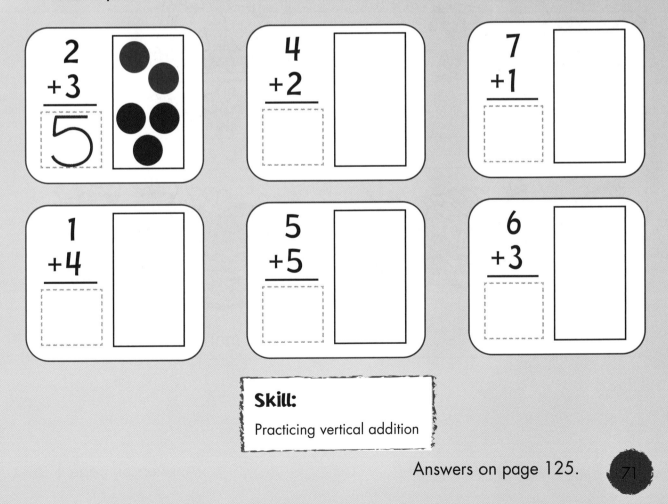

$$\begin{array}{r} 2 \\ +3 \\ \hline 5 \end{array}$$

$$\begin{array}{r} 4 \\ +2 \\ \hline \end{array}$$

$$\begin{array}{r} 7 \\ +1 \\ \hline \end{array}$$

$$\begin{array}{r} 1 \\ +4 \\ \hline \end{array}$$

$$\begin{array}{r} 5 \\ +5 \\ \hline \end{array}$$

$$\begin{array}{r} 6 \\ +3 \\ \hline \end{array}$$

Skill:

Practicing vertical addition

Answers on page 125.

How Many Are Left?

Subtracting is taking away. You subtract to find out how many are left.

7 ducks
2 go away
5 ducks are left

Count to find out how many are left.

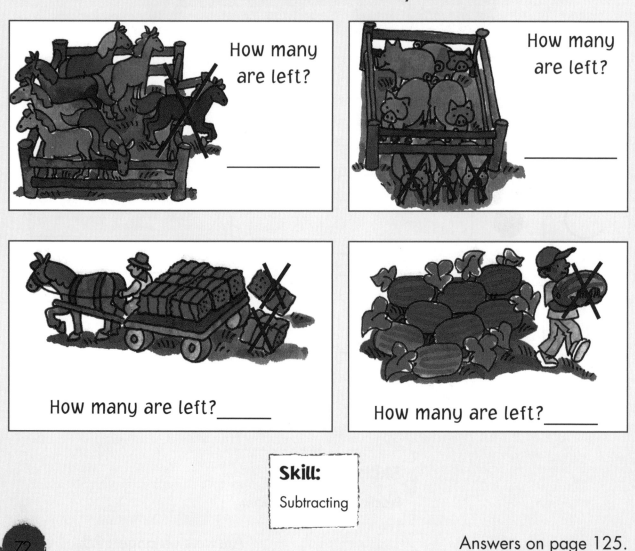

How many are left? _____

How many are left? _____

How many are left? _____

How many are left? _____

Skill:

Subtracting

72

Answers on page 125.

Number Sentences

7	minus	2	is	5
7	−	2	=	5

Count the chicks. Take away the ones that are crossed out.
Tell how many are left.

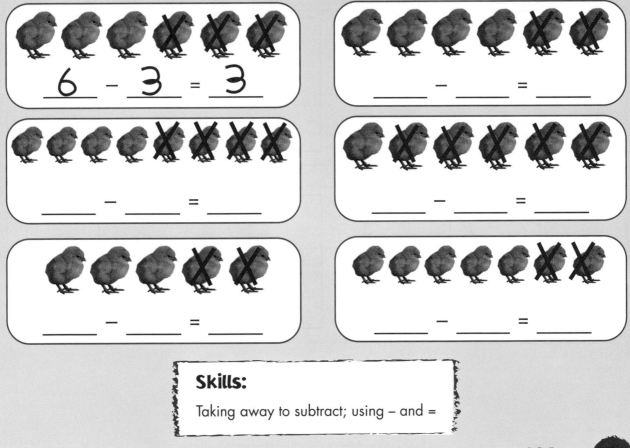

6 − 3 = 3

___ − ___ = ___

___ − ___ = ___

___ − ___ = ___

___ − ___ = ___

___ − ___ = ___

Skills:

Taking away to subtract; using − and =

Answers on page 125.

Another Way to Subtract

These number facts have the same answer.

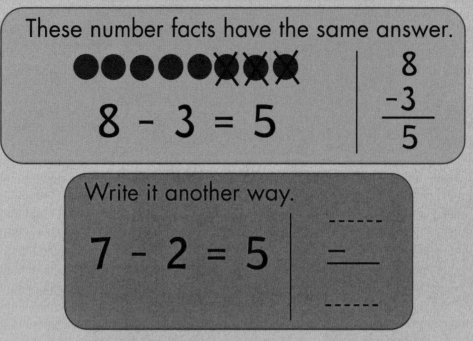

8 - 3 = 5

$$\begin{array}{r} 8 \\ -3 \\ \hline 5 \end{array}$$

Write it another way.

7 - 2 = 5

$$\begin{array}{r} ------ \\ -- \\ \hline \\ ------ \end{array}$$

Make a picture to show the numbers. Subtract to tell how many are left.

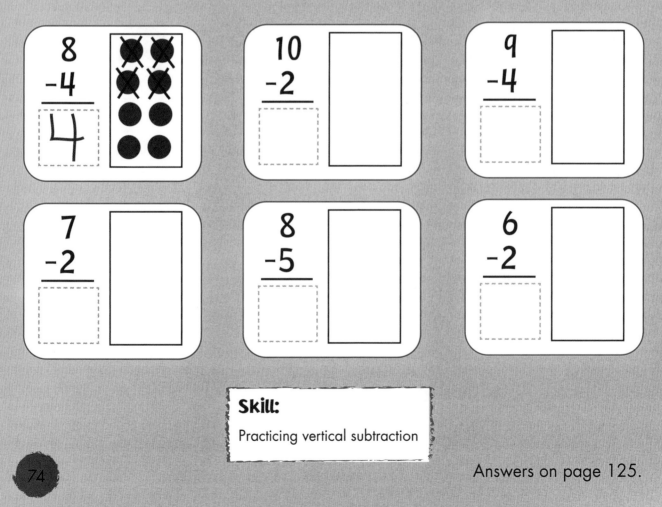

$$\begin{array}{r} 8 \\ -4 \\ \hline 4 \end{array}$$

$$\begin{array}{r} 10 \\ -2 \\ \hline \end{array}$$

$$\begin{array}{r} 9 \\ -4 \\ \hline \end{array}$$

$$\begin{array}{r} 7 \\ -2 \\ \hline \end{array}$$

$$\begin{array}{r} 8 \\ -5 \\ \hline \end{array}$$

$$\begin{array}{r} 6 \\ -2 \\ \hline \end{array}$$

Skill:

Practicing vertical subtraction

Answers on page 125.

Look at the Signs

When you see + , add the numbers.

When you see − , subtract the numbers.

BUMPER CARS

5 + 2 = _____

7 − 3 = _____

GET YOUR TICKETS

8 + 1 = _____

6 − 3 = _____

SEE THE BABY DUCKS

4 + 4 = _____

7 − 0 = _____

COUNTY FAIR

FAMILY DAY

```
  9     5
 -4    +3
____   ____
```

```
  2     8
 +6    -7
____   ____
```

Skill:

Adding and subtracting to 10

Answers on page 125.

Meet a Number Family!

Adding and subtracting are opposites.

$3 + 1 = 4$ $4 - 1 = 3$

1, 3, and 4 are a number family. Here are the number sentences in the family.

$$1 + 3 = 4 \qquad 4 - 1 = 3$$
$$3 + 1 = 4 \qquad 4 - 3 = 1$$

Finish the number sentences for each number family.

1, 2, 3
$1 + 2 = $ ____ $3 - 1 = $ ____
$2 + 1 = $ ____ $3 - 2 = $ ____

2, 3, 5
$2 + 3 = $ ____ $5 - 2 = $ ____
$3 + 2 = $ ____ $5 - 3 = $ ____

2, 1, 1
$1 + 1 = $ ____
$2 - 1 = $ ____

0, 5, 5
$0 + 5 = $ ____ $5 + 0 = $ ____
$5 - 0 = $ ____ $5 - 5 = $ ____

1, 4, 5
$1 + 4 = $ ____ $5 - 1 = $ ____
$4 + 1 = $ ____ $5 - 4 = $ ____

2, 2, 4
$2 + 2 = $ ____
$4 - 2 = $ ____

Parents:

Help your child realize that knowing addition facts helps with subtraction facts. They just have to think of the numbers in the number family. If $2 + 2 = 4$, then $4 - 2 = 2$, the other number in the number family.

Skills:

Working with number families; inverse relationship of addition and subtraction

Answers on page 125.

Jam-Packed With Numbers!

Finish the number families.

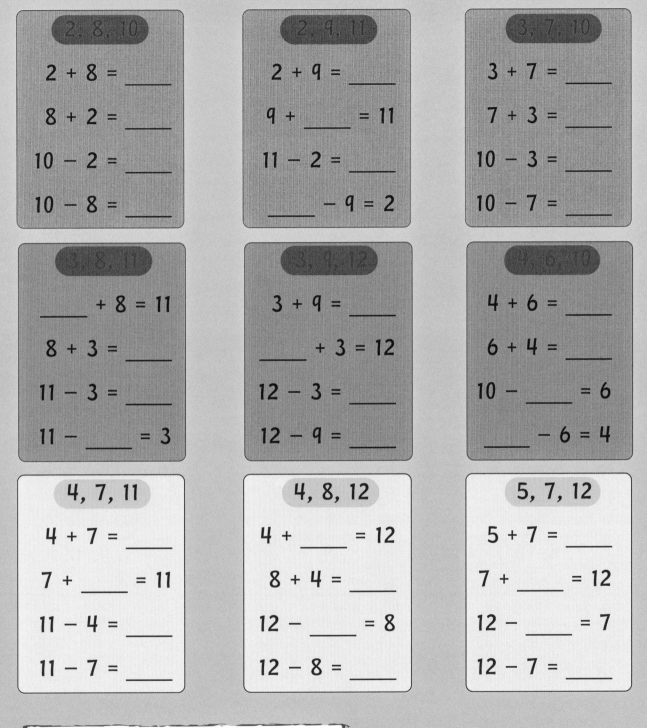

2, 8, 10

2 + 8 = _____

8 + 2 = _____

10 − 2 = _____

10 − 8 = _____

2, 9, 11

2 + 9 = _____

9 + _____ = 11

11 − 2 = _____

_____ − 9 = 2

3, 7, 10

3 + 7 = _____

7 + 3 = _____

10 − 3 = _____

10 − 7 = _____

3, 8, 11

_____ + 8 = 11

8 + 3 = _____

11 − 3 = _____

11 − _____ = 3

3, 9, 12

3 + 9 = _____

_____ + 3 = 12

12 − 3 = _____

12 − 9 = _____

4, 6, 10

4 + 6 = _____

6 + 4 = _____

10 − _____ = 6

_____ − 6 = 4

4, 7, 11

4 + 7 = _____

7 + _____ = 11

11 − 4 = _____

11 − 7 = _____

4, 8, 12

4 + _____ = 12

8 + 4 = _____

12 − _____ = 8

12 − 8 = _____

5, 7, 12

5 + 7 = _____

7 + _____ = 12

12 − _____ = 7

12 − 7 = _____

Skill:

Working with number families to 15

Family Finish!

Finish the number families.

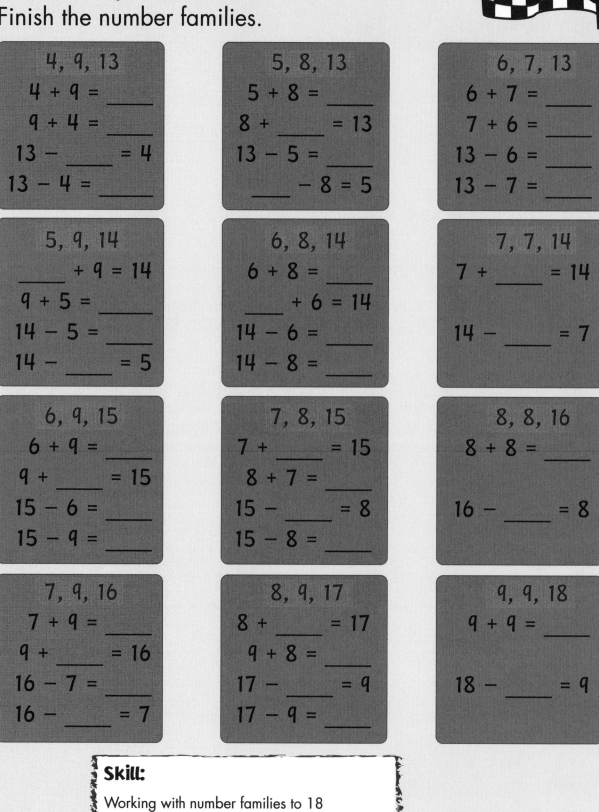

4, 9, 13

4 + 9 = _____

9 + 4 = _____

13 − _____ = 4

13 − 4 = _____

5, 8, 13

5 + 8 = _____

8 + _____ = 13

13 − 5 = _____

_____ − 8 = 5

6, 7, 13

6 + 7 = _____

7 + 6 = _____

13 − 6 = _____

13 − 7 = _____

5, 9, 14

_____ + 9 = 14

9 + 5 = _____

14 − 5 = _____

14 − _____ = 5

6, 8, 14

6 + 8 = _____

_____ + 6 = 14

14 − 6 = _____

14 − 8 = _____

7, 7, 14

7 + _____ = 14

14 − _____ = 7

6, 9, 15

6 + 9 = _____

9 + _____ = 15

15 − 6 = _____

15 − 9 = _____

7, 8, 15

7 + _____ = 15

8 + 7 = _____

15 − _____ = 8

15 − 8 = _____

8, 8, 16

8 + 8 = _____

16 − _____ = 8

7, 9, 16

7 + 9 = _____

9 + _____ = 16

16 − 7 = _____

16 − _____ = 7

8, 9, 17

8 + _____ = 17

9 + 8 = _____

17 − _____ = 9

17 − 9 = _____

9, 9, 18

9 + 9 = _____

18 − _____ = 9

Skill:

Working with number families to 18

Answers on page 126.

Hit the Target

How fast can you add? Ask someone to time you.

9 + 1	5 + 3	2 + 6	7 + 3	8 + 2
☐	☐	☐	☐	☐

2 + 7	4 + 3	8 + 1	5 + 0	2 + 3
☐	☐	☐	☐	☐

5 + 4	7 + 2	6 + 2	3 + 3	4 + 4
☐	☐	☐	☐	☐

6 + 1	3 + 7	5 + 2	9 + 0	2 + 4
☐	☐	☐	☐	☐

It took me

_____

minutes to finish the page.

I got

_____

facts right.

Parents:

You may want to photocopy this page so your child can complete it more than once, trying to improve time and accuracy.

Skill:

Adding with sums to 10: timed

Answers on page 126.

Fair Facts

How fast can you subtract?
Ask someone to time you.

9 − 2	8 − 4	9 − 5	7 − 1	5 − 3
6 − 3	10 − 1	7 − 2	6 − 2	8 − 6
8 − 2	6 − 5	7 − 5	5 − 2	4 − 3
10 − 7	7 − 4	5 − 1	10 − 2	9 − 1

It took me

_____

minutes to finish the page.

I got

_____

facts right.

Parents:

You may want to photocopy this page so your child can complete it more than once, trying to improve time and accuracy.

Skill:

Subtracting with differences to 10: timed

Answers on page 126.

Missing Numbers

Write the number that is missing in each number sentence.

COUNTY FAIR

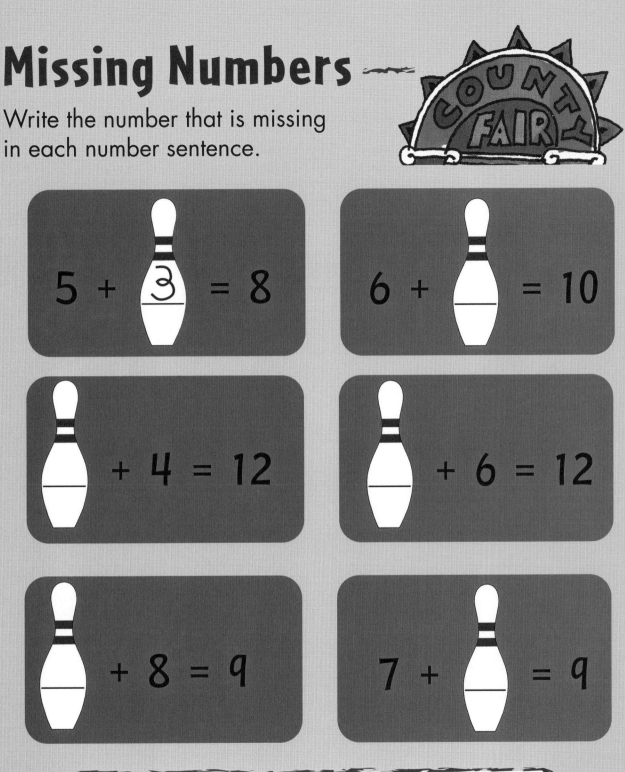

5 + 3 = 8

6 + ☐ = 10

☐ + 4 = 12

☐ + 6 = 12

☐ + 8 = 9

7 + ☐ = 9

Answers on page 126.

Fact Toss!

$$16 - 9 = \boxed{}$$

$$2 + 9 = \boxed{}$$

$$4 + 7 = \boxed{}$$

$$16 - 8 = \boxed{}$$

$$10 - 3 = \boxed{}$$

$$5 + 6 = \boxed{}$$

$$11 - 9 = \boxed{}$$

$$6 + 8 = \boxed{}$$

$$4 + 8 = \boxed{}$$

$$6 + 7 = \boxed{}$$

Skill:

Adding and subtracting to 18

82

Check for + and – to see if you add or subtract. Then write the answers in the square.

14	18	12	5	3
− 8	− 9	− 6	+ 9	+ 9

13	3	6	13	17
− 8	+ 8	+ 9	− 9	− 8

Answers on page 126.

Addition Towers

When you have three numbers to add, add two numbers first.
Then add the third number.

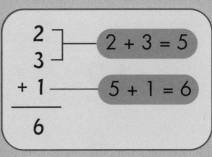

```
 2 ┐
   ├──  2 + 3 = 5
 3 ┘
+ 1 ─────  5 + 1 = 6
───
 6
```

Add these numbers.

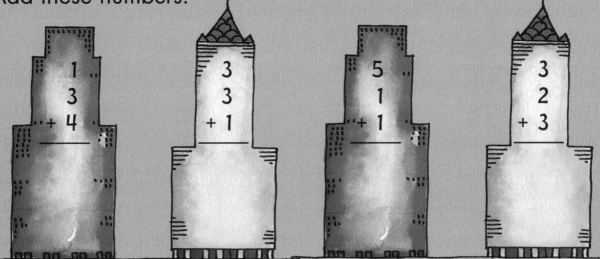

```
  1          3          5          3
  3          3          1          2
+ 4        + 1        + 1        + 3
────       ────       ────       ────
```

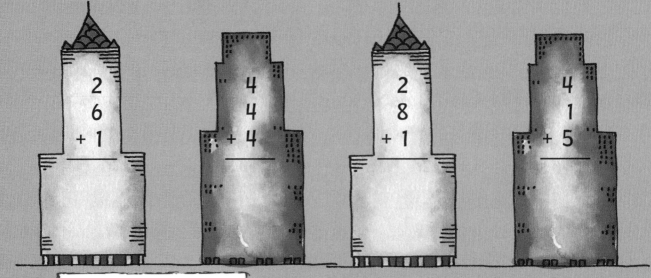

```
  2          4          2          4
  6          4          8          1
+ 1        + 4        + 1        + 5
────       ────       ────       ────
```

Skill:

Adding three numbers

84

Answers on page 126.

Addition Stories

Read the stories. Add to find the answers.

There are 4 red trucks on the road. There are 5 blue trucks. How many trucks are there in all?

4 trucks
+ 5 trucks
9 trucks

The store has 7 big windows and 3 little windows. How many windows are there in all?

windows
+ windows
windows

The pet shop has 6 orange fish and 3 black fish. How many fish are there all together?

fish
+ fish
fish

Ana got 5 books at the store. Tony gave her 2 more books. How many books does Ana have in all?

books
+ books
books

Tony saw 3 dogs at the park. He saw 6 more dogs on the way home. How many dogs did Tony see in all?

dogs
+ dogs
dogs

Skill:

Solving addition word problems

Answers on page 126.

Subtraction Stories

Read the stories. Subtract to find the answers.

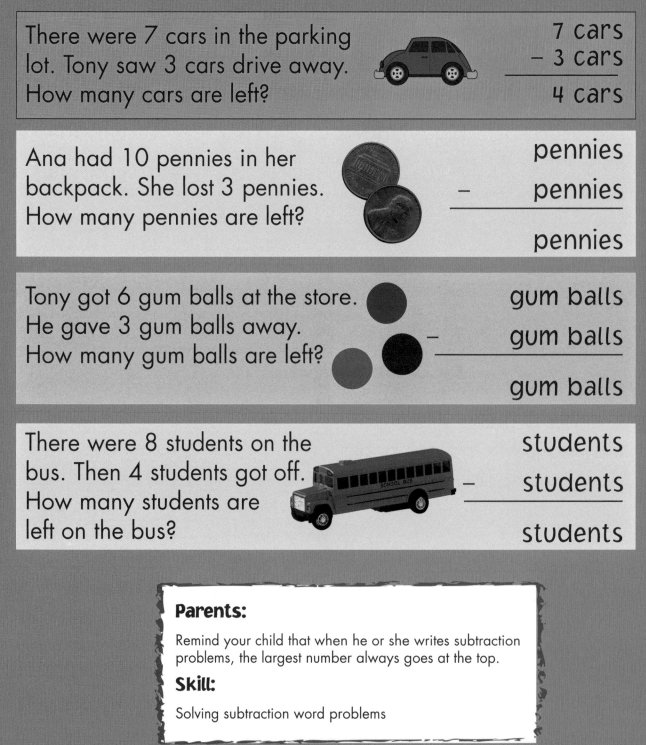

There were 7 cars in the parking lot. Tony saw 3 cars drive away. How many cars are left?

7 cars
– 3 cars
4 cars

Ana had 10 pennies in her backpack. She lost 3 pennies. How many pennies are left?

_____ pennies
– _____ pennies
_____ pennies

Tony got 6 gum balls at the store. He gave 3 gum balls away. How many gum balls are left?

_____ gum balls
– _____ gum balls
_____ gum balls

There were 8 students on the bus. Then 4 students got off. How many students are left on the bus?

_____ students
– _____ students
_____ students

Parents:

Remind your child that when he or she writes subtraction problems, the largest number always goes at the top.

Skill:

Solving subtraction word problems

Answers on page 126.

Find Your Seat!

The rodeo is starting! Look at the ticket to find your seat. First find the row. Then find the seat in that row.

	Seat 1	Seat 2	Seat 3	Seat 4	Seat 5
Row 1					
Row 2					
Row 3					
Row 4					
Row 5					

Find the seat. Color it red. Row 2, Seat 3

Find the seat. Color it blue. Row 1, Seat 4

Find the seat. Color it black. Row 3, Seat 2

Find the seat. Color it green. Row 2, Seat 5

Find the seat. Color it yellow. Row 3, Seat 3

Find the seat. Color it purple. Row 4, Seat 1

Find the seat. Color it brown. Row 5, Seat 5

Find the seat. Color it pink. Row 5, Seat 2

Skill:

Locating coordinates on a grid

Answers on page 126.

Find the Sum

The arrow shows you how to find the sum for 2 + 3.

+	1	2	3	4	5	6	7	8	9
1	2	3	4	5	6	7	8	9	10
2	3	4	5	6	7	8	9	10	11
3	4	⑤	6	7	8	9	10	11	12
4	5	6	7	8	9	10	11	12	13
5	6	7	8	9	10	11	12	13	14
6	7	8	9	10	11	12	13	14	15
7	8	9	10	11	12	13	14	15	16
8	9	10	11	12	13	14	15	16	17
9	10	11	12	13	14	15	16	17	18

Use the chart to find these sums.

Find the sum of 6 + 2. Color the square red.

Find the sum of 3 + 8. Color the square green.

Find the sum of 4 + 6. Color the square blue.

Find the sum of 7 + 8. Color the square pink.

Find the sum of 4 + 9. Color the square yellow.

Find the sum of 5 + 8. Color the square orange.

Find the sum of 6 + 5. Put **X** in the square.

Find the sum of 8 + 8. Circle the sum.

Parents:

Provide more practice by saying an addition fact and having your child find the intersection of the grid that has the sum.

Skill:

Using an addition grid to add

Answers on page 126.

Subtraction Fun

Addition and subtraction are opposites. So you can use the chart to find answers when you subtract too!

+	1	2	3	4	5	6	7	8	9
1	2	3	4	5	6	7	8	9	10
2	3	4	5	6	7	8	9	10	11
3	4	5	6	7	8	9	10	11	12
4	5	6	7	8	9	10	11	12	13
5	6	7	8	9	10	11	12	13	14
6	7	8	9	10	11	12	13	14	15
⑦	8	9	10	11	12	13	14	15	16
8	9	10	11	12	13	14	15	16	17
9	10	11	12	13	14	15	16	17	18

Find the answer for 10 – 3.

First find 3 on the top line. Go down to 10. Then go all the way across to the left. The answer is circled.

10 – 3 = 7

Use the chart to find the answers.

18 – 9 = _____   12 – 4 = _____

16 – 7 = _____   11 – 3 = _____

14 – 6 = _____   13 – 7 = _____

10 – 4 = _____   15 – 8 = _____

14 – 5 = _____   16 – 9 = _____

Skill:

Using an addition grid to subtract

Answers on page 126.

Rodeo Facts

Rugged Deals

When you see + , add the numbers.

When you see − , subtract the numbers.

$4 + 5 =$ _____ $10 − 9 =$ _____ $6 + 3 =$ _____

$7 − 3 =$ _____ $2 + 7 =$ _____ $10 − 4 =$ _____

$$\begin{array}{r} 10 \\ -\ 6 \\ \hline \end{array} \qquad \begin{array}{r} 5 \\ +\ 3 \\ \hline \end{array} \qquad \begin{array}{r} 8 \\ +\ 1 \\ \hline \end{array} \qquad \begin{array}{r} 9 \\ -\ 7 \\ \hline \end{array} \qquad \begin{array}{r} 4 \\ +\ 3 \\ \hline \end{array}$$

$$\begin{array}{r} 9 \\ -\ 2 \\ \hline \end{array} \qquad \begin{array}{r} 6 \\ +\ 4 \\ \hline \end{array} \qquad \begin{array}{r} 1 \\ +\ 5 \\ \hline \end{array} \qquad \begin{array}{r} 10 \\ -\ 0 \\ \hline \end{array}$$

Skill:

Reviewing mixed addition and subtraction to 10

Answers on page 126.

More Rodeo Facts

When you see + , add the numbers.

When you see − , subtract the numbers.

4 + 8 = _____   18 − 9 = _____   6 + 6 = _____

12 − 3 = _____   8 + 7 = _____   11 − 4 = _____

15 − 6	5 + 7	8 + 6	16 − 7

4 + 9	17 − 8

9 + 3	4 + 5

Skill:

Reviewing mixed addition and subtraction to 18

Answers on page 126.

Fast Facts!

How fast can you add? Ask someone to time you.

$$7 + 9$$ $$6 + 5$$ $$8 + 7$$ $$7 + 5$$ $$5 + 8$$

$$6 + 8$$ $$8 + 3$$ $$7 + 4$$ $$9 + 9$$ $$7 + 7$$

$$5 + 9$$ $$5 + 6$$ $$4 + 8$$ $$6 + 6$$ $$8 + 5$$

$$7 + 8$$ $$8 + 6$$ $$9 + 4$$ $$7 + 6$$ $$9 + 8$$

$$6 + 9$$ $$9 + 6$$ $$8 + 9$$ $$5 + 7$$ $$6 + 7$$

It took me

_____

minutes to finish the page.

I got _____ facts right.

Parents:

You may want to photocopy this page so your child can complete it more than once, trying to improve time and accuracy.

Skill:

Adding sums to 18: timed

Answers on page 126.

More Fast Facts

How fast can you subtract? Ask someone to time you.

16 − 8	13 − 7	15 − 9	14 − 8	17 − 9
11 − 6	15 − 6	14 − 5	13 − 6	12 − 5
17 − 8	13 − 5	12 − 4	18 − 9	16 − 9
15 − 8	16 − 7	14 − 7	12 − 8	13 − 9
13 − 8	14 − 6	11 − 7	12 − 6	15 − 7

It took me

_____

minutes to finish the page.

I got _____ facts right.

Parents:

You may want to photocopy this page so your child can complete it more than once, trying to improve time and accuracy.

Skill:

Subtracting differences to 18: timed

Answers on page 126.

Plus and Minus Clues

Add when you see these words: How many in all? How many all together? **Subtract** when you see these words: How many are left? How many more? How many less?

Read each problem. Write your answer in the box.

There are 6 cows and 8 horses in the barn. How many animals are there in all?

Each cow needs 10 bales of hay a week. Each horse needs 12 bales of hay. How many more bales does a horse need?

The cowgirl has 6 ropes. The cowboy has 4 ropes. How many ropes do they have all together?

Parents:

You may want to read the story problems with your child.

Skill:

Solving word problems: mixed addition and subtraction

The rodeo clown moved 14 barrels. The cowhand moved 6 barrels. How many more barrels did the clown move?

There were 5 boys sitting on the fence. There were 7 girls. How many children were sitting on the fence in all?

One judge gave out 5 blue ribbons and 8 red ribbons. How many ribbons did the judge give all together?

Another judge gave 12 red ribbons and 5 blue ribbons. How many more red ribbons did the judge give?

Eight cowhands tried to ride the biggest bull. Six of them fell off. How many are left on the bull?

If one man has 6 tickets and another man has 5 tickets, how many tickets do they have all together?

Answers on page 127.

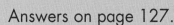

Round-Off Time!

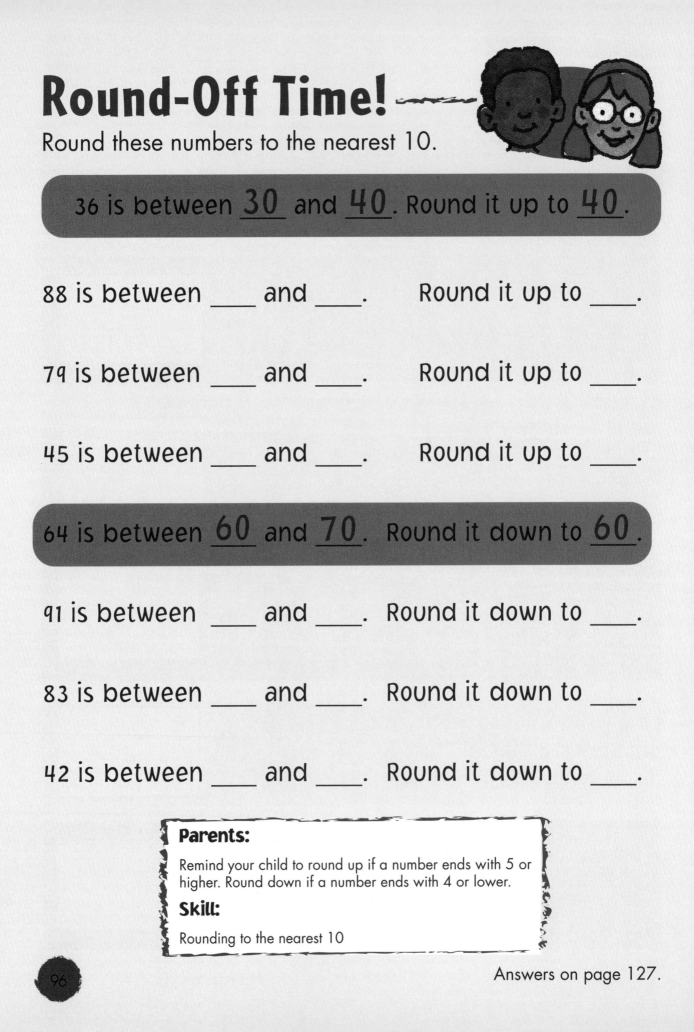

Round these numbers to the nearest 10.

36 is between __30__ and __40__. Round it up to __40__.

88 is between ___ and ___.   Round it up to ___.

79 is between ___ and ___.   Round it up to ___.

45 is between ___ and ___.   Round it up to ___.

64 is between __60__ and __70__. Round it down to __60__.

91 is between ___ and ___. Round it down to ___.

83 is between ___ and ___. Round it down to ___.

42 is between ___ and ___. Round it down to ___.

Parents:

Remind your child to round up if a number ends with 5 or higher. Round down if a number ends with 4 or lower.

Skill:

Rounding to the nearest 10

Answers on page 127.

Take a Guess

When you make a good guess, you are **estimating.**
Estimate how many animals are in each group.

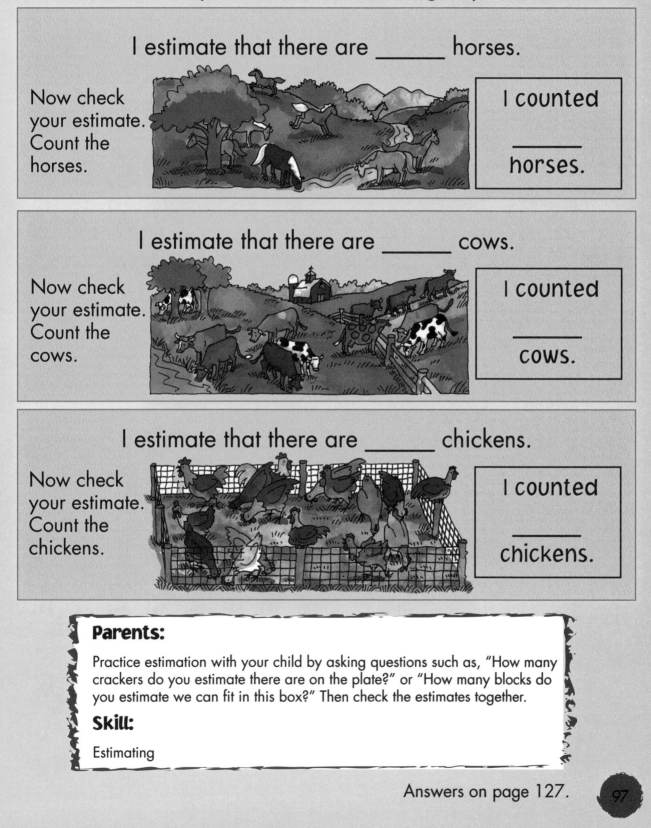

I estimate that there are _____ horses.

Now check your estimate. Count the horses.

I counted _____ horses.

I estimate that there are _____ cows.

Now check your estimate. Count the cows.

I counted _____ cows.

I estimate that there are _____ chickens.

Now check your estimate. Count the chickens.

I counted _____ chickens.

Parents:

Practice estimation with your child by asking questions such as, "How many crackers do you estimate there are on the plate?" or "How many blocks do you estimate we can fit in this box?" Then check the estimates together.

Skill:

Estimating

Answers on page 127.

Pens of 10

Draw circles to put the chicks into pens with 10 chicks in each pen. Write how many sets of 10 you have. Then write how many chicks are left over in each group. The first one is done for you.

Sets of 10	Ones left over
2	3

Sets of 10	Ones left over

Sets of 10	Ones left over

Skill:

Making groups of 10

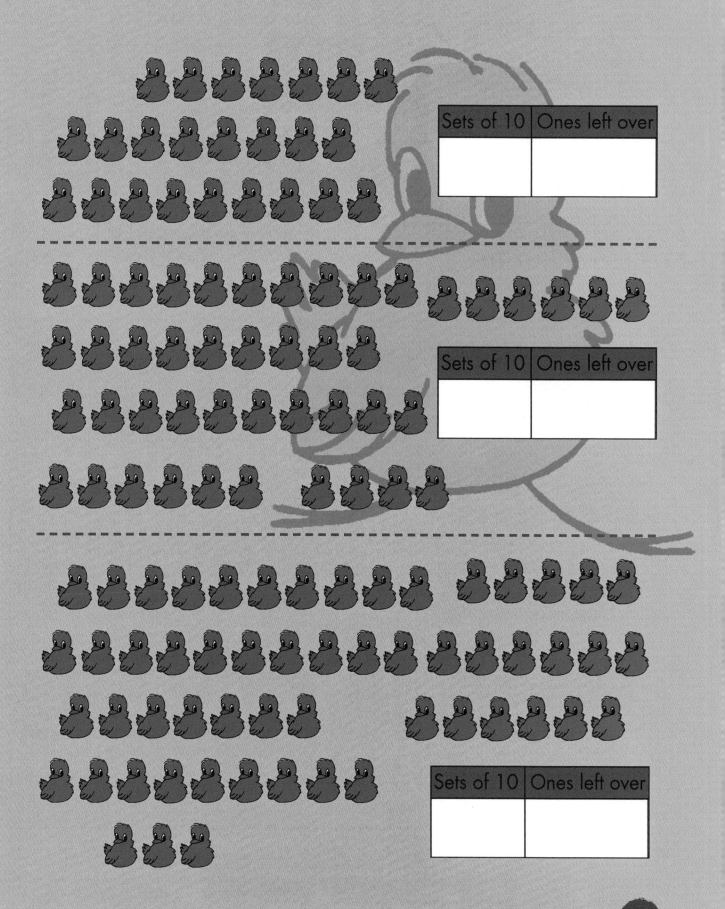

Sets of 10	Ones left over

Sets of 10	Ones left over

Sets of 10	Ones left over

Answers on page 127.

Tens and Ones

tens	ones	
4	2	$42 = 4$ tens $+ 2$ ones

Tell how many tens and how many ones.

65 = _____ tens + _____ ones

84 = _____ tens + _____ ones

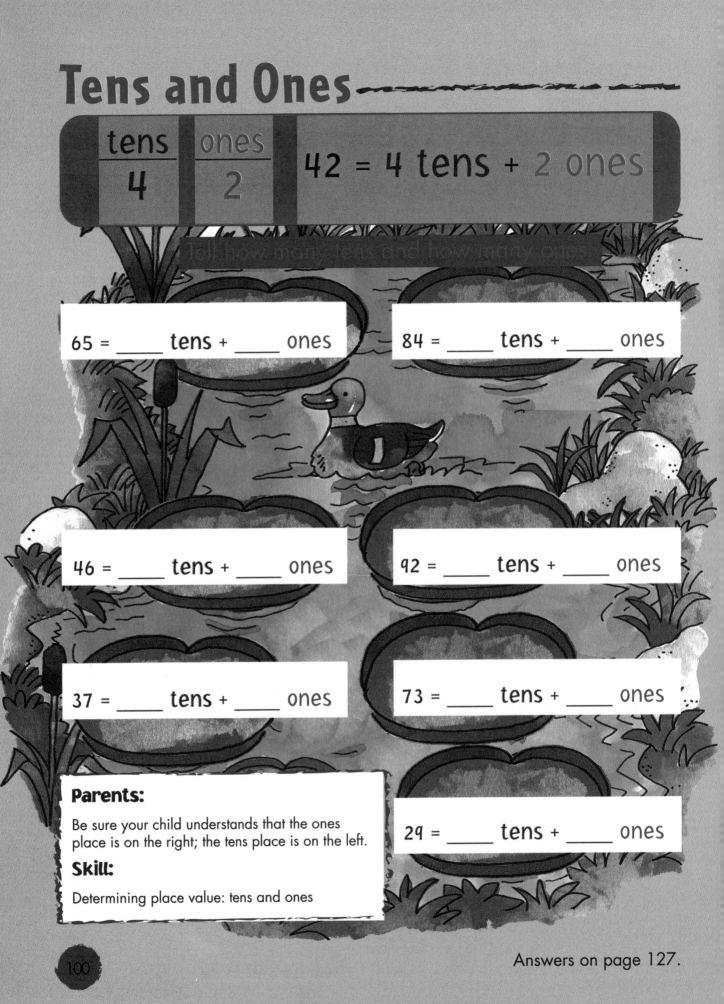

46 = _____ tens + _____ ones

92 = _____ tens + _____ ones

37 = _____ tens + _____ ones

73 = _____ tens + _____ ones

Parents:

Be sure your child understands that the ones place is on the right; the tens place is on the left.

Skill:

Determining place value: tens and ones

29 = _____ tens + _____ ones

Answers on page 127.

Number Stretching

tens	ones	Stretch it out!
4	2	$42 = 40 + 2$

24 = _____ + _____

79 = _____ + _____

36 = _____ + _____

43 = _____ + _____

67 = _____ + _____

84 = _____ + _____

92 = _____ + _____

51 = _____ + _____

Parents:

You may want to review counting by 10s with your child before doing this activity.

Skill:

Understanding expanded notation

Answers on page 127.

Shoe Values

Write the number on each shoe.

45
4 tens + 5 ones

3 tens + 2 ones

4 tens + 0 ones

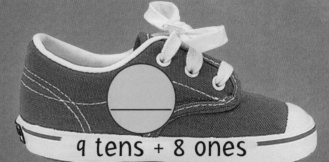
9 tens + 8 ones

6 tens + 1 one

7 tens + 2 ones

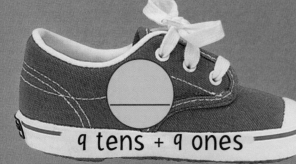
9 tens + 9 ones

5 tens + 4 ones

Skill:

Reviewing place value

Answers on page 127.

Adding Things Up!

Add the ones first.	Then add the tens.
42 + 21 —— 3	42 + 21 —— 63

$$
\begin{array}{r} 32 \\ + 11 \\ \hline \end{array}
\qquad
\begin{array}{r} 25 \\ + 13 \\ \hline \end{array}
\qquad
\begin{array}{r} 22 \\ + 40 \\ \hline \end{array}
$$

$$
\begin{array}{r} 61 \\ + 10 \\ \hline \end{array}
\qquad
\begin{array}{r} 43 \\ + 43 \\ \hline \end{array}
\qquad
\begin{array}{r} 80 \\ + 12 \\ \hline \end{array}
$$

$$
\begin{array}{r} 16 \\ + 41 \\ \hline \end{array}
\qquad
\begin{array}{r} 28 \\ + 21 \\ \hline \end{array}
\qquad
\begin{array}{r} 54 \\ + 23 \\ \hline \end{array}
$$

$$
\begin{array}{r} 45 \\ + 20 \\ \hline \end{array}
\qquad
\begin{array}{r} 72 \\ + 22 \\ \hline \end{array}
\qquad
\begin{array}{r} 41 \\ + 34 \\ \hline \end{array}
$$

Skill:

Adding 2-digit numbers without regrouping

Spidery Subtraction

Subtract the ones first.	Then subtract the tens.
58 − 13 ―― 5	58 − 13 ―― 45

```
  99          65          56
- 22        - 12        - 20
----        ----        ----
```

```
  47          88          71
- 23        - 43        - 60
----        ----        ----
```

```
  23          57          98
- 13        - 35        - 76
----        ----        ----
```

```
  34          64          77
- 21        - 52        - 45
----        ----        ----
```

Skill:

Subtracting 2-digit numbers without regrouping

Answers on page 127.

Monkey Math

Add or subtract. If an answer equals 25, color the space yellow. What do you see?

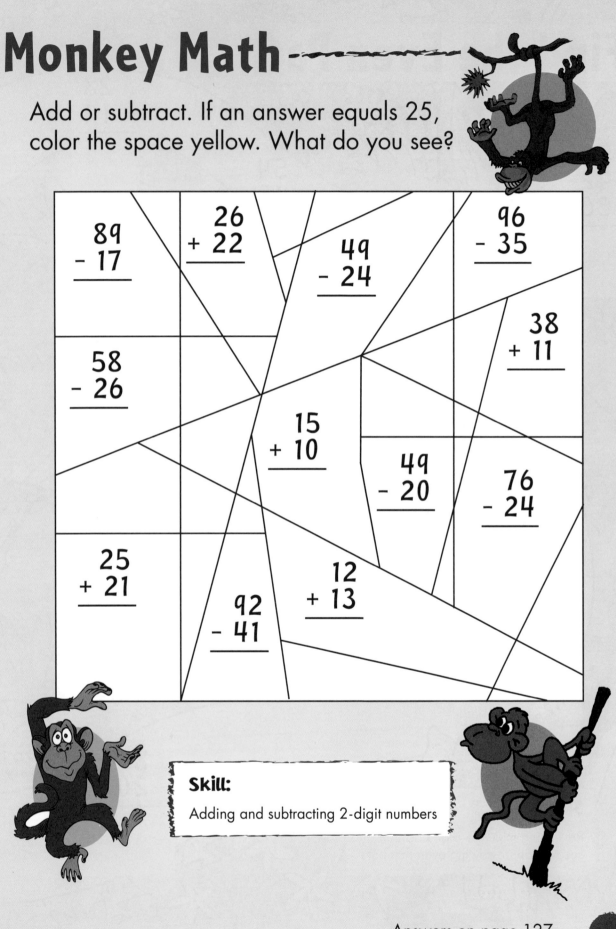

$$89 - 17$$

$$26 + 22$$

$$49 - 24$$

$$96 - 35$$

$$58 - 26$$

$$38 + 11$$

$$15 + 10$$

$$49 - 20$$

$$76 - 24$$

$$25 + 21$$

$$92 - 41$$

$$12 + 13$$

Skill:

Adding and subtracting 2-digit numbers

Find the Even Path

$$28 - 11$$

$$42 + 36$$

$$71 + 21$$

$$54 + 15$$

$$63 - 21$$

$$65 + 10$$

$$95 - 13$$

$$62 + 14$$

$$84 - 20$$

Skill:

Reviewing mixed 2-digit addition and subtraction; reviewing even numbers

Add or subtract. Then circle the answers that are even numbers. Follow the even numbers to the river.

55
− 22

49
− 12

76
+ 21

87
− 25

70
+ 26

At the Toy Store

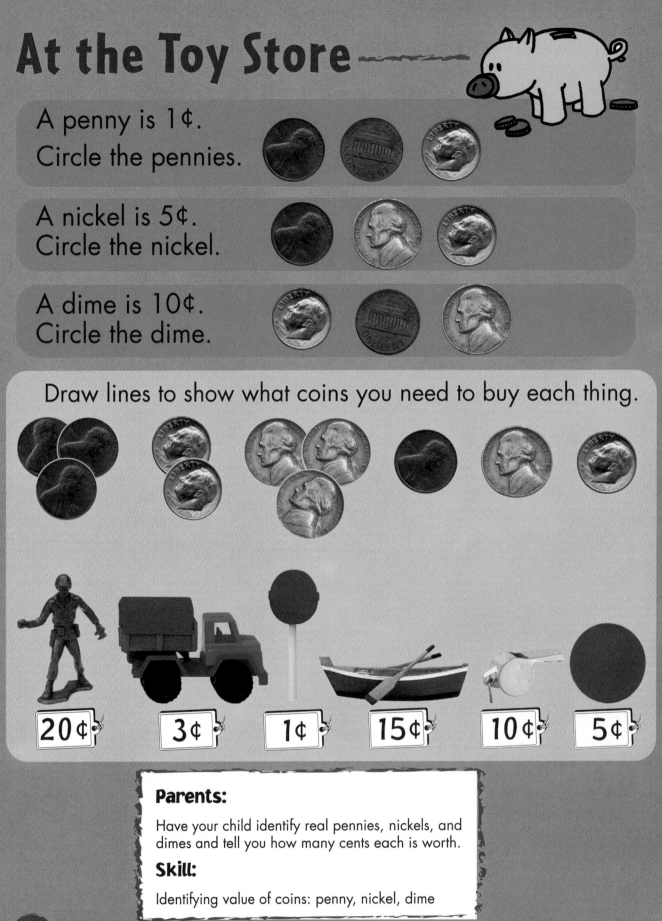

A penny is 1¢.
Circle the pennies.

A nickel is 5¢.
Circle the nickel.

A dime is 10¢.
Circle the dime.

Draw lines to show what coins you need to buy each thing.

| 20¢ | 3¢ | 1¢ | 15¢ | 10¢ | 5¢ |

Parents:

Have your child identify real pennies, nickels, and dimes and tell you how many cents each is worth.

Skill:

Identifying value of coins: penny, nickel, dime

Answers on page 128.

At the Grocery Store

quarter
25¢

half-dollar
50¢

Circle each thing you could buy with one quarter.

22¢    36¢ 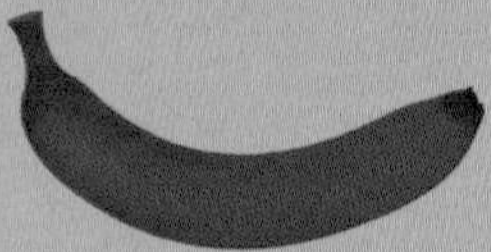   15¢

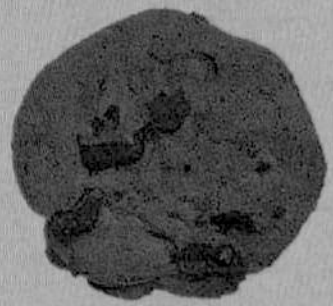

24¢    53¢    20¢

Circle each thing you could buy with one half-dollar.

45¢    38¢    75¢

50¢    89¢    49¢

Skill:

Identifying value of coins: quarter, half-dollar

Answers on page 128.

At the Bank

Trade in your coins.

Draw lines to match coins that are worth the same amount. You can use some answers twice.

Skill:

Understanding coin equivalencies

Answers on page 128.

At the Pet Store

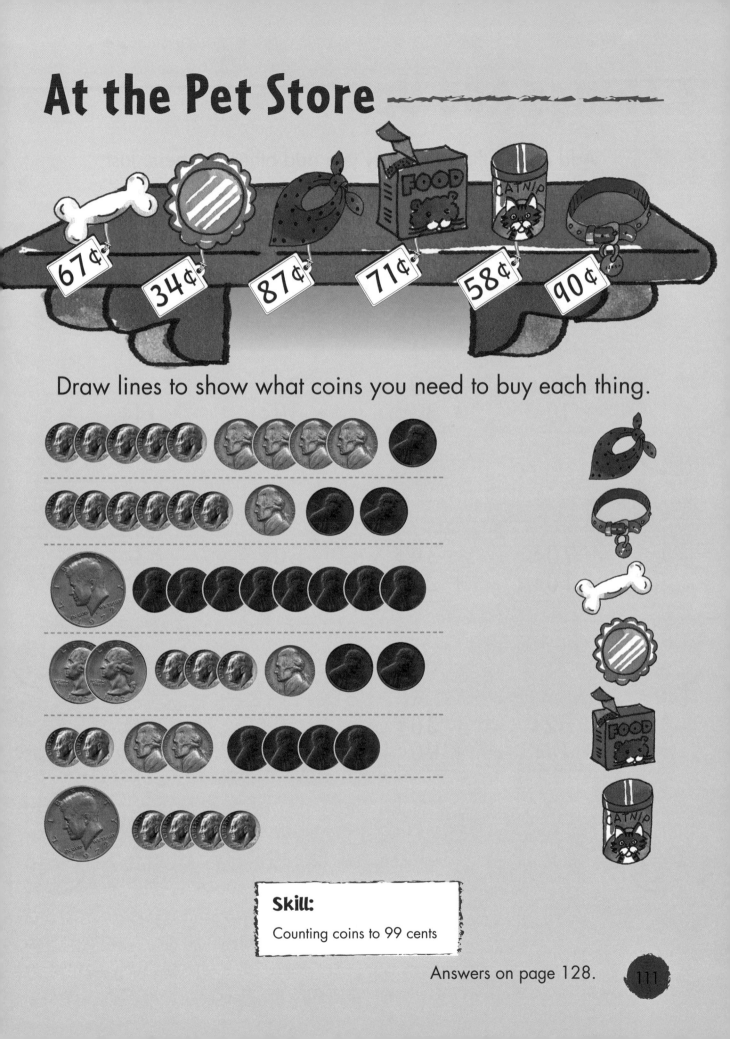

Draw lines to show what coins you need to buy each thing.

Skill:

Counting coins to 99 cents

Things Add Up!

Add money the same way you add other numbers. Just remember to put a cents sign (¢) in your answer.

$$\begin{array}{r} 15¢ \\ + 40¢ \\ \hline 55¢ \end{array}$$

$\begin{array}{r} 50¢ \\ + 10¢ \\ \hline \end{array}$	$\begin{array}{r} 30¢ \\ + 33¢ \\ \hline \end{array}$	$\begin{array}{r} 21¢ \\ + 34¢ \\ \hline \end{array}$	$\begin{array}{r} 67¢ \\ + 11¢ \\ \hline \end{array}$
$\begin{array}{r} 70¢ \\ + 10¢ \\ \hline \end{array}$	$\begin{array}{r} 34¢ \\ + 22¢ \\ \hline \end{array}$	$\begin{array}{r} 50¢ \\ + 25¢ \\ \hline \end{array}$	$\begin{array}{r} 63¢ \\ + 12¢ \\ \hline \end{array}$
$\begin{array}{r} 52¢ \\ + 11¢ \\ \hline \end{array}$	$\begin{array}{r} 30¢ \\ + 40¢ \\ \hline \end{array}$	$\begin{array}{r} 10¢ \\ + 15¢ \\ \hline \end{array}$	$\begin{array}{r} 63¢ \\ + 15¢ \\ \hline \end{array}$

Skill:

Adding money using cents sign

Answers on page 128.

Take the Money!

Subtract money the same way you subtract other numbers.
Just remember to put a cents sign (¢) in your answer.

$$
\begin{array}{r}
48¢ \\
- 27¢ \\
\hline
21¢
\end{array}
$$

40¢ − 10¢	77¢ − 23¢	68¢ − 34¢	89¢ − 13¢
66¢ − 30¢	25¢ − 12¢	55¢ − 22¢	63¢ − 42¢
42¢ − 21¢	54¢ − 30¢	33¢ − 11¢	54¢ − 10¢

Skill:

Subtracting money using cents sign

Answers on page 128.

Dollar Days

dollar $1.00

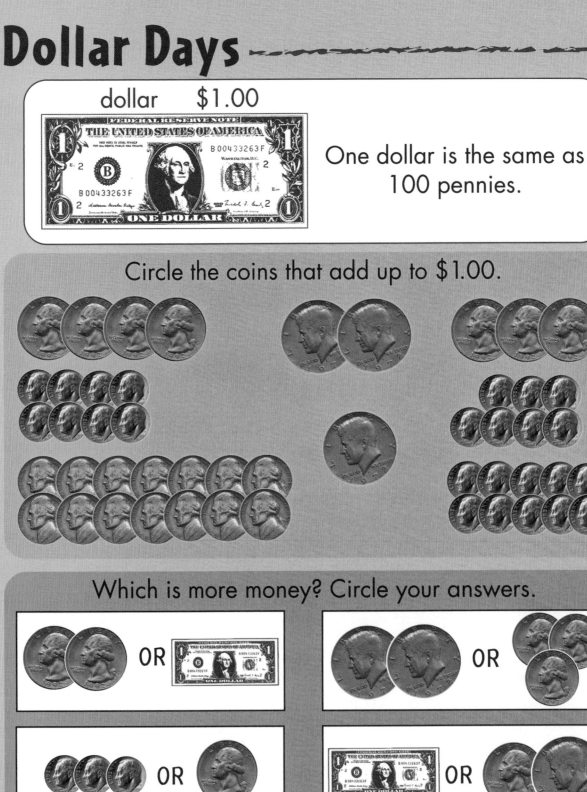

One dollar is the same as 100 pennies.

Circle the coins that add up to $1.00.

Which is more money? Circle your answers.

OR

OR

OR

OR

Skill:

Recognizing the value of a dollar bill

114

Answers on page 128.

Dollars and Cents

You can put dollars and cents together!

$1.25 is 1 dollar and 25 cents | $2.40 is 2 dollars and 40 cents

Draw lines to show how much money you need for each treat.

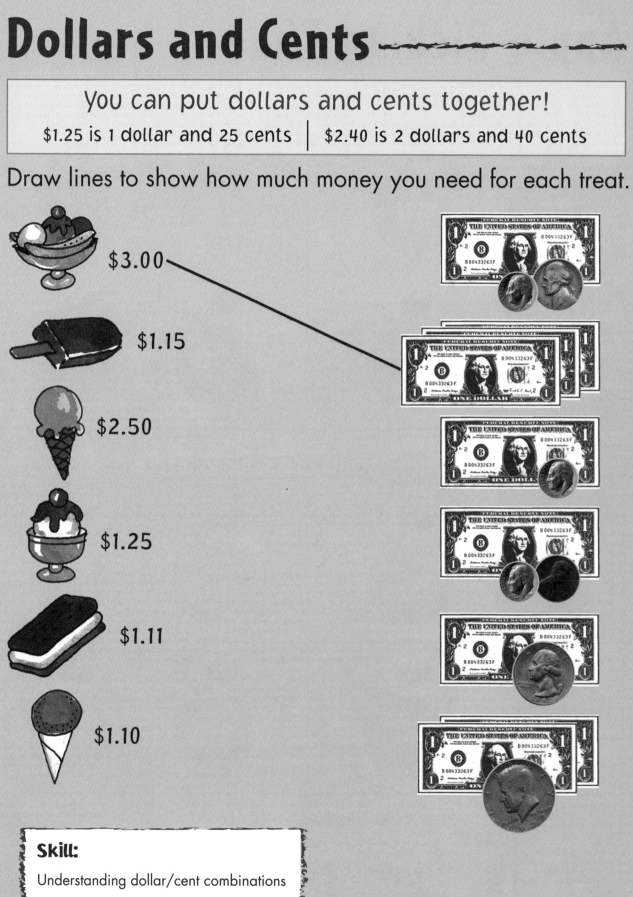

$3.00

$1.15

$2.50

$1.25

$1.11

$1.10

Skill:

Understanding dollar/cent combinations

Answers on page 128.

Apple-Picking Time

Circle the apple with the number that is greater.

45 or 54

29 or 26

81 or 79

75 or 71

Circle the apple with the number that is less.

99 or 87

47 or 74

90 or 89

35 or 48

Skill:

Understanding greater than/less than (2-digit numbers)

116

Answers on page 128.

Greater or Less?

> means **greater than**	< means **less than**
10 > 8	8 < 10
10 is greater than 8	8 is less than 10

Write > or < to compare the numbers.

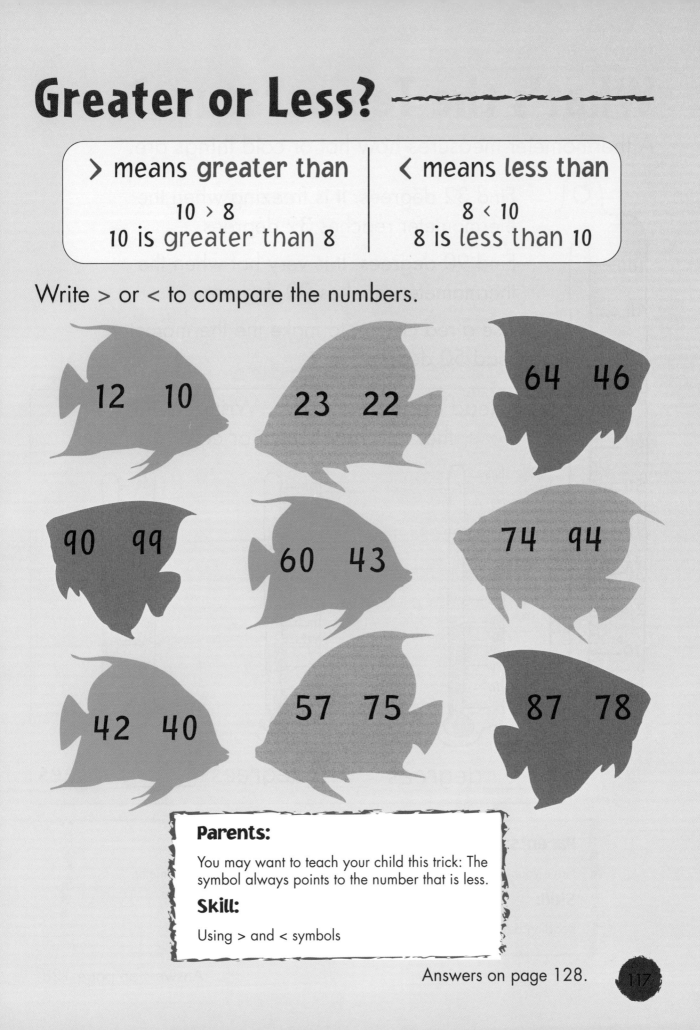

12   10

23   22

64   46

90   99

60   43

74   94

42   40

57   75

87   78

Parents:

You may want to teach your child this trick: The symbol always points to the number that is less.

Skill:

Using > and < symbols

Answers on page 128.

What's the Temperature?

A thermometer measures how hot or cold things are.

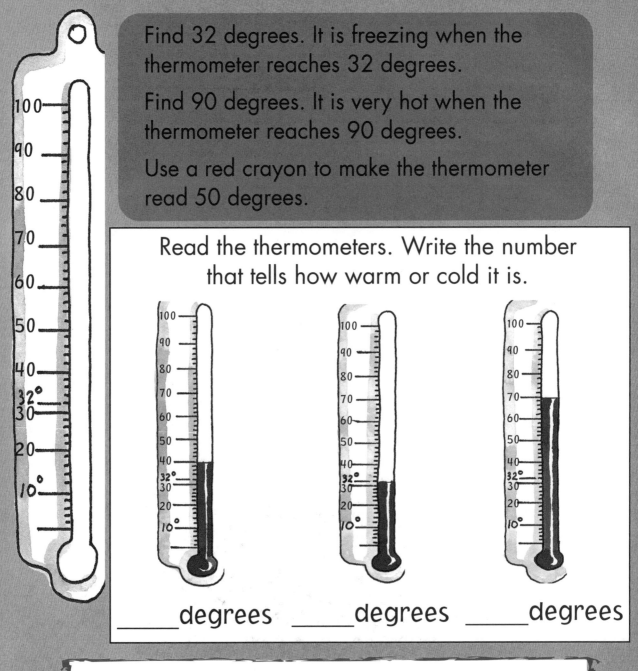

Find 32 degrees. It is freezing when the thermometer reaches 32 degrees.

Find 90 degrees. It is very hot when the thermometer reaches 90 degrees.

Use a red crayon to make the thermometer read 50 degrees.

Read the thermometers. Write the number that tells how warm or cold it is.

_____ degrees   _____ degrees   _____ degrees

Parents:

Have your child practice reading the temperature on a real thermometer.

Skill:

Reading a thermometer

Answers on page 128.

Falling for Tens and Ones

Tell how many tens and how many ones.

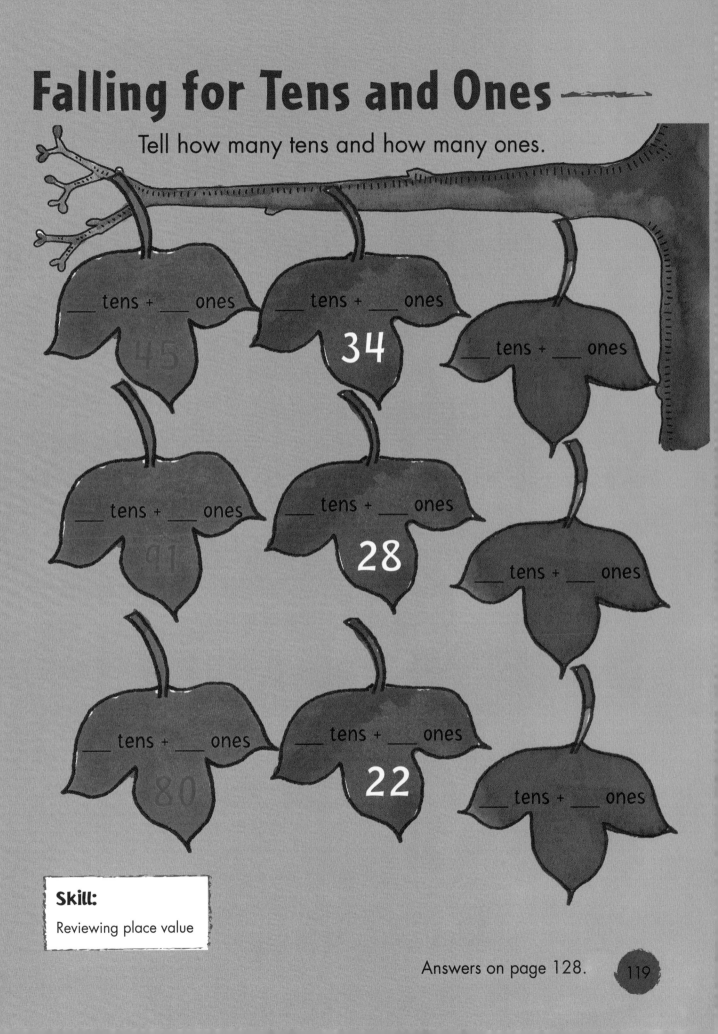

___ tens + ___ ones

45

___ tens + ___ ones

34

___ tens + ___ ones

___ tens + ___ ones

91

___ tens + ___ ones

28

___ tens + ___ ones

___ tens + ___ ones

80

___ tens + ___ ones

22

___ tens + ___ ones

Skill:

Reviewing place value

Answers on page 128.

Three at a Time

Can you count by 3s? Write the missing numbers.

3   6   ___   12   ___   18

21   24   ___   30   ___   36

30   33   36   ___   42   ___

52   55   ___   61   ___   ___

Skill:

Counting by 3s

120

Answers on page 128.

Answer Pages

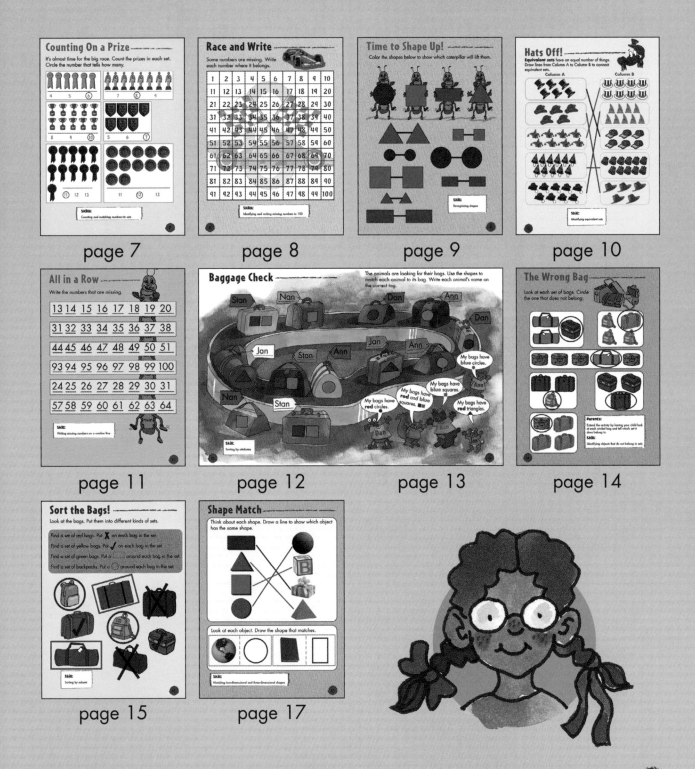

page 7

page 8

page 9

page 10

page 11

page 12

page 13

page 14

page 15

page 17

page 18

page 19

page 20

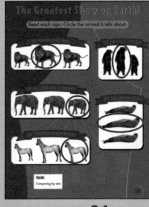
page 21

page 22

page 23

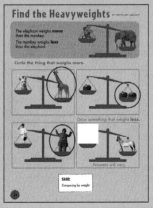
page 24

page 25

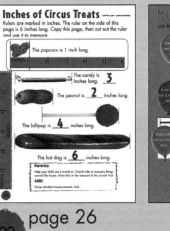
page 26

page 27

page 28

page 29

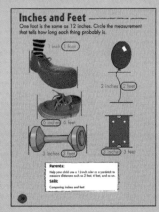

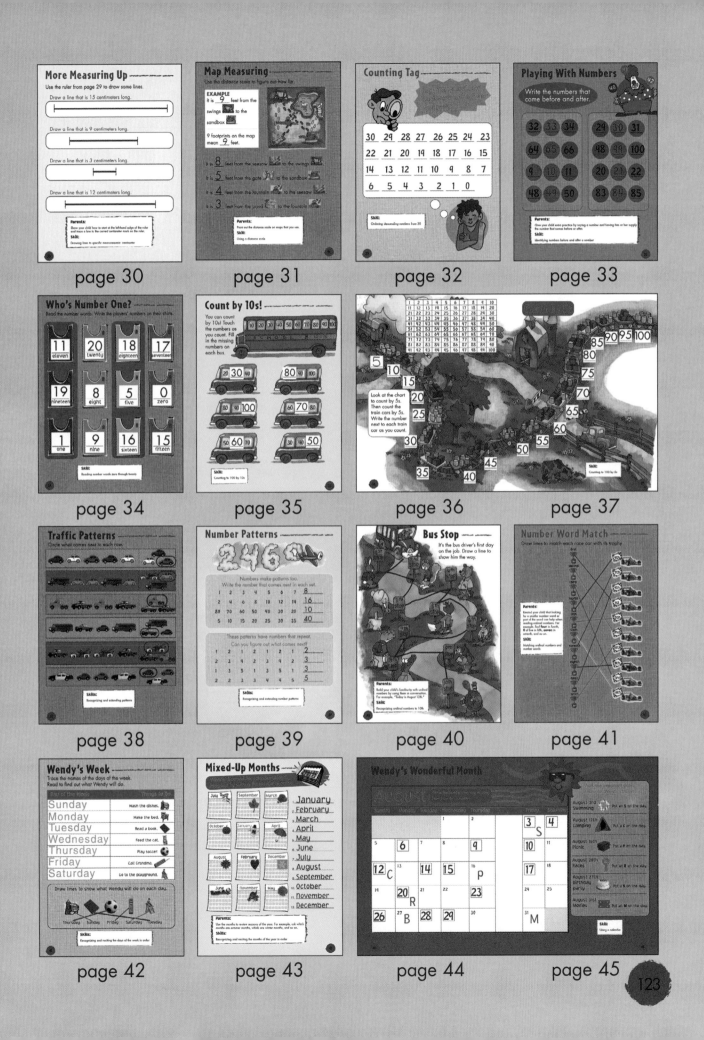

page 30

page 31

page 32

page 33

page 34

page 35

page 36

page 37

page 38

page 39

page 40

page 41

page 42

page 43

page 44

page 45

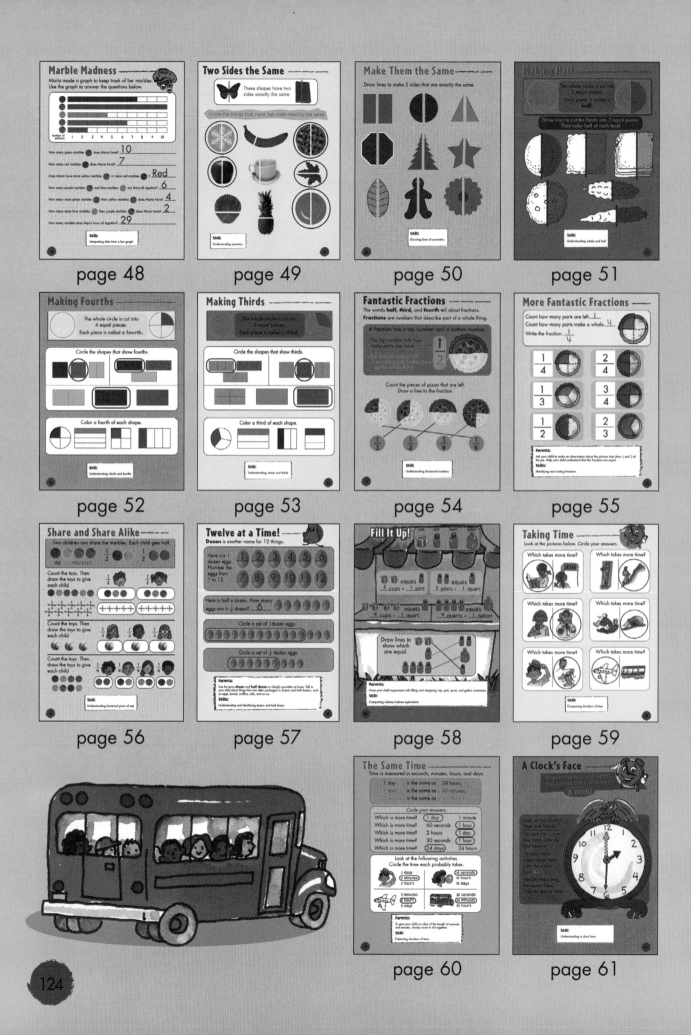

page 48

page 49

page 50

page 51

page 52

page 53

page 54

page 55

page 56

page 57

page 58

page 59

page 60

page 61

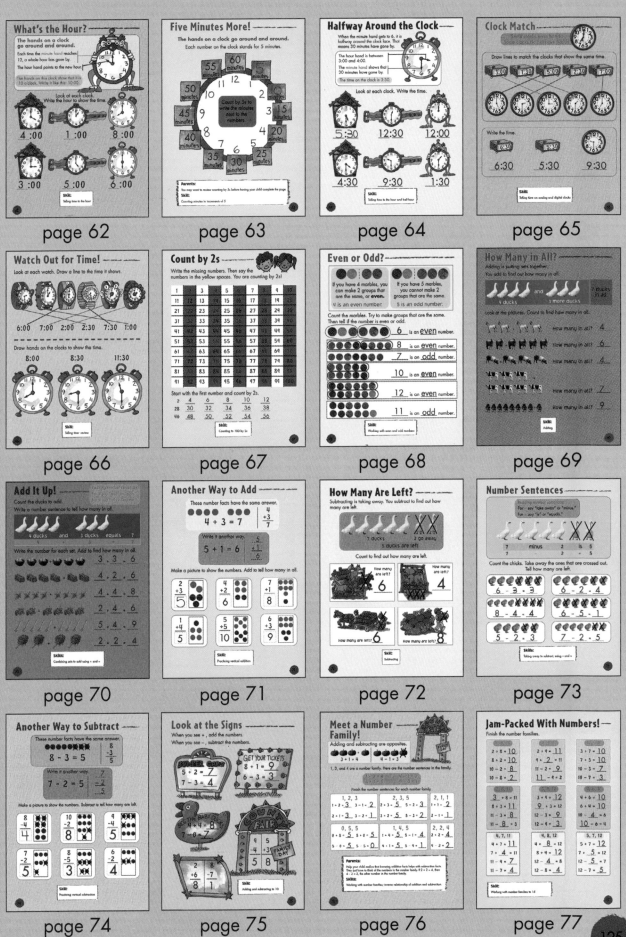

page 62

page 63

page 64

page 65

page 66

page 67

page 68

page 69

page 70

page 71

page 72

page 73

page 74

page 75

page 76

page 77

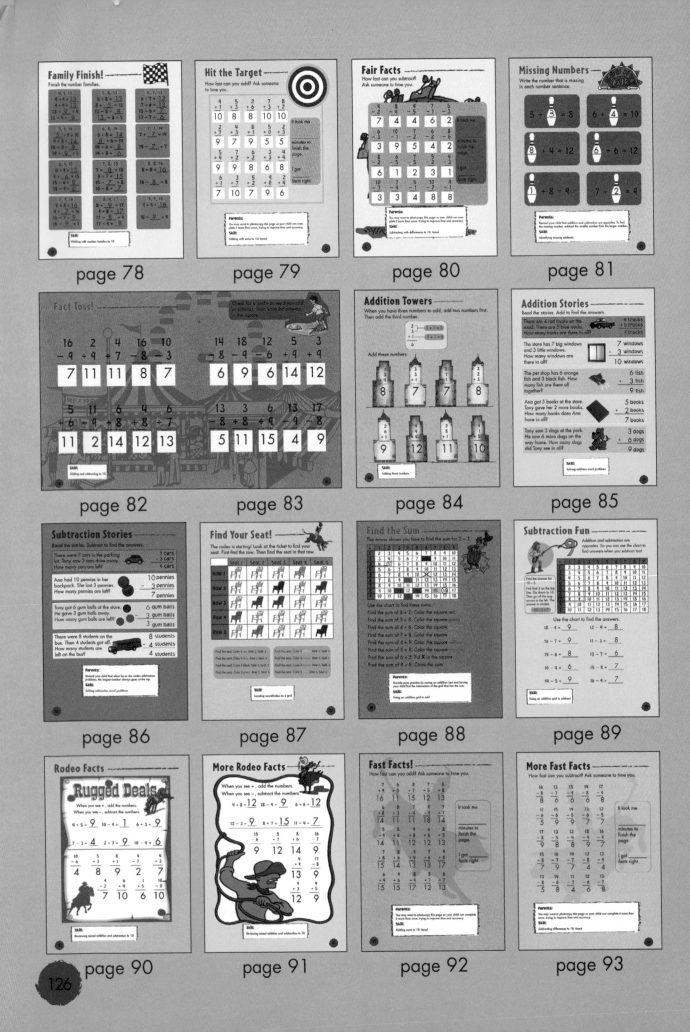

page 78

page 79

page 80

page 81

page 82

page 83

page 84

page 85

page 86

page 87

page 88

page 89

page 90

page 91

page 92

page 93

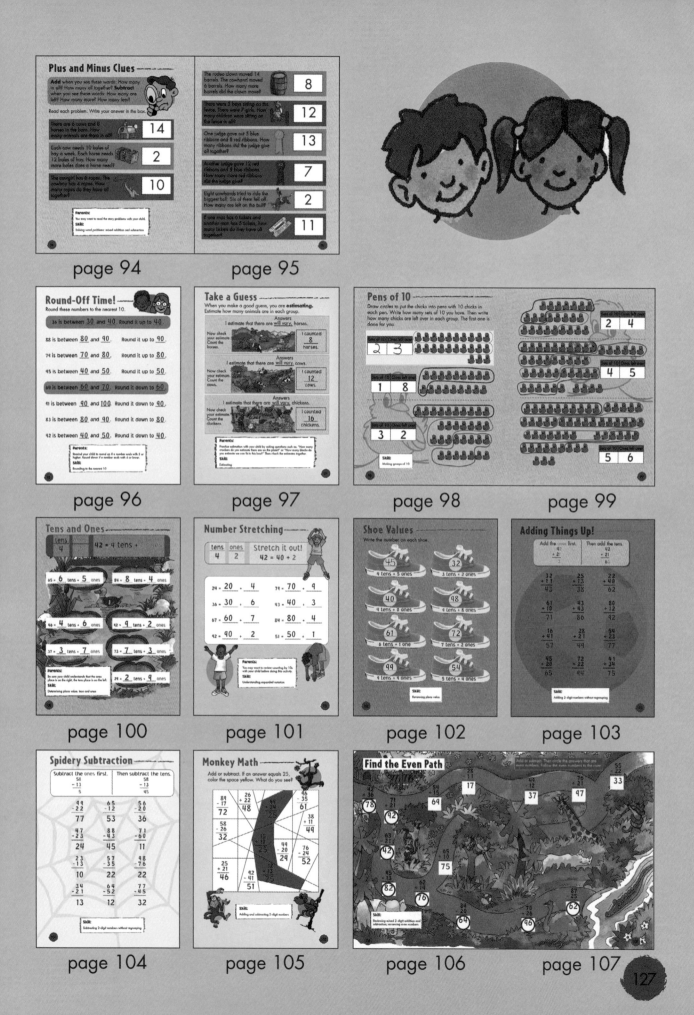

page 94

page 95

page 96

page 97

page 98

page 99

page 100

page 101

page 102

page 103

page 104

page 105

page 106

page 107

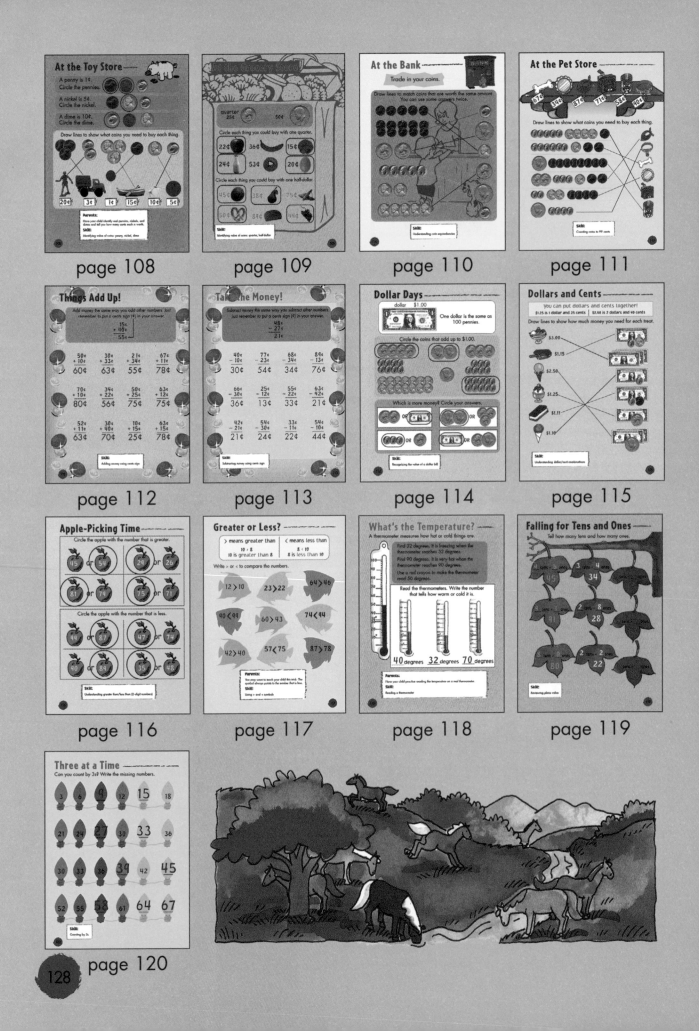

page 108

page 109

page 110

page 111

page 112

page 113

page 114

page 115

page 116

page 117

page 118

page 119

page 120